HANGED AT
WINCHESTER

STEVE FIELDING

The History Press

First published 2010

The History Press
The Mill, Brimscombe Port
Stroud, Gloucestershire, GL5 2QG
www.thehistorypress.co.uk

British Library Cataloguing in Publication Data.
A catalogue record for this book is available from the British Library.

ISBN 978 0 7524 5707 9

Typesetting and origination by The History Press
Printed in Great Britain
Manufacturing managed by Jellyfish Print Solutions Ltd

CONTENTS

ABOUT THE AUTHOR

Steve Fielding was born in Bolton, Lancashire, in the 1960s. He attended Bolton County Grammar School and served an apprenticeship as an engineer before embarking on a career as a professional musician. After many years of recording and touring, both in Great Britain and Europe, he began writing in 1993 and had his first book published a year later. He is the author of over a twenty books on the subject of true crime, and in particular hangmen and executions.

Hanged at Winchester is the seventh in a series and follows *Hanged at Birmingham*, *Hanged at Leeds*, *Hanged at Manchester*, *Hanged at Pentonville*, *Hanged at Liverpool* and *Hanged at Durham*. He compiled the first complete study of modern-day executions, *The Hangman's Record 1868-1964*, and, as well as writing a number of regional murder casebooks, is also the author of two recent books on executioners: *Pierrepoint: A Family of Executioners* and *The Executioner's Bible – Hangmen of the 20th Century*. He has regularly contributed to magazines including the *Criminologist*, *Master Detective* and *True Crime* and has worked as Historical Consultant on the Discovery Channel series *The Executioners*, and *Executioner: Pierrepoint* for the Crime & Investigation channel. He has also appeared on *Dead Strange* (Southern Television), BBC1's *The One Show*, and *Most Haunted Live* on the Living TV channel. Besides writing he also teaches at a local college.

ACKNOWLEDGEMENTS

I would like to thank the following people for help with this book. Firstly to Lisa Moore for her help in every stage in the production, but mainly with the photographs and proofreading. I offer my sincere thanks again to both Tim Leech and Matthew Spicer, who have been willing to share information along with rare documents, photographs and illustrations from their own collections. I would also like to acknowledge the help given by Janet Buckingham who helped to input the original data. Finally, I would like to acknowledge the generous help with information and photographs given by Alan Constable.

PREVIOUS TITLES IN THE SERIES

RESEARCH MATERIALS AND SOURCES

As with my other books on capital punishment and executions, many people have supplied information and photographs over the years, some of whom have since passed away. I remain indebted to the help with rare photographs and material given to me by the late Syd Dernley (assistant executioner) and the late Frank McKue (former prison officer).

The bulk of the research for this book was done many years ago and extra information has been added to my database as and when it has become available. In most instances contemporary local and national newspapers have supplied the basic information, which has been supplemented by material found in PCOM, HO and ASSI files held at the National Record Office at Kew, and the Home Office Capital Case File 1901-1948. Other information is in the author's collection pertaining to a number of those directly involved in some of the cases.

Space doesn't permit a full bibliography of books and websites accessed while researching this project, but one book in particular, *Five Wings and a Tower: Winchester Prison 1850-2002* proved to be an excellent reference work on the history of the prison, and is worthy of a mention. I have tried to locate the copyright owners of all images used in this book, but a number of them were untraceable. In particular, I been unable to locate the copyright holders of a number of images, in the main those sourced from the National Archives. I apologise if I have inadvertently infringed any existing copyright.

Steve Fielding, April 2010
www.stevefielding.com

INTRODUCTION

HMP Winchester, situated on Romsey Road, has housed many notable inmates since it opened in 1849. It was the main gaol for felons convicted of offences not just in Hampshire and its neighbouring counties, but occasionally from much further afield. This has included modernist poet, Quaker and pacifist Basil Cheesman Bunting, arrested as a conscientious objector after voicing his opposition to the First World War in 1918; Keith Mann, a high-ranking member of the Animal Liberation Front, sentenced to fourteen years imprisonment in 1994, for setting fire to lorries carrying meat; notorious lifer Charles Bronson; and mass murderer Rose West, who was held here in 1995.

The city of Winchester has had a prison since the thirteenth century. At various times it had been situated in the High Street and the castle, but in 1228 it was located on a site between Staple Gardens and Jewry Street. A new county gaol was constructed in 1788 and in 1805 a new debtor's prison was also built in Jewry Street. Designed by well-known architect George Moneypenny, the building eventually cost over £10,000 and its imposing appearance was heavily criticised in 1817 as it was deemed far too opulent to house common criminals. Jewry Street was also renamed Gaol Street around this time, but, following complaints from local residents, its name soon reverted back.

In 1845, a committee of magistrates was appointed to decide if a new prison was required. Agreeing that it was, work began in 1846 on the site on Romsey Road. Architect Charles Pearce was appointed to design and build the new prison, having previously built the new gaol at Aylesbury. Construction soon ran into difficulty, however, and Pearce and his Clerk of Works were dismissed and Thomas Stopher, a local builder, was brought in to complete the project.

The building was completed and ready for inmates in September 1849, although problems with the water supply meant that the transfers were not completed until December. Prisoners were brought in from Jewry Street Gaol and also bridewells in Winchester, Southampton, Portsmouth and Gosport. Although three of the bridewells (a miniature type of prison comprising of a small number of cells usually in a police station or town hall) were closed following the opening of Winchester Gaol, the one at Gosport remained open to deal with large numbers of service men frequently being imprisoned there.

In common with other prisons of the era, the gaol was constructed in the classical Victorian 'radial', based around the Panopticon concept that had originated in the American penal system before being adopted across Europe. The design of having a

The main gate of Winchester Prison. (Alan Constable)

central tower with wings attached like spokes radiating from a hub allowed a warder to have a clear view down each wing from the one central location. The new prison covered an area of over six acres, with five wings, each of four stories high, radiating from a centre, which houses a prominent ventilation tower, visible for miles around. The tower contains a system of ducting installed to supply fresh air which remains effective into the twenty-first century.

Each wing was built with a large window at the gable end at the height of two storeys, and each cell had a gas burner to supplement the natural light from the windows. There were large skylights in the pitched roof, which let in natural light, while water for the prison was obtained from a 217ft-deep well in the grounds, which was estimated to use over 9,000 gallons per day. Running water was installed in 1896 but it was to be almost a century later, in 1993, when integral sanitation was completed and did away with the archaic practice of 'slopping out'.

The prison also housed a treadmill that could accommodate almost fifty prisoners at a time, and cells were fitted with hand cranks, a box with a handle that had to be turned by the prisoner. Serving no purpose whatsoever, the prisoner could be punished by being made to take a number of turns on the handle. A warder could adjust the resistance by turning a screw on the side of the box, thus controlling the amount of effort needed to turn the handle, a legacy of which is why, even today, prison officers are known as 'screws'.

A report in July 1871 stated that the prison was able to hold 321 males and 31 female prisoners, along with the capacity for 29 male and 4 female debtors, held in a separate building in the prison grounds. The daily average prisoner population was 316 but by 1899 this number had risen to 345. Today the operational maximum capacity is 721. A Prison Reform Trust in August 2003 reported that overcrowding at Winchester Prison was an ongoing problem. Over half of the prisoners were sharing cells which were designed for one person and there had been three suicides in the previous year. In April 2005, another inspection report from Her Majesty's Chief Inspector of Prisons stated that Winchester was still overcrowded and prisoners did not have enough work to do. The report also stated that vulnerable inmates were not well protected and relations between staff and prisoners were not good.

There had been a number of changes to the prison during its history: in 1908 a hospital was built within the prison walls, despite the Royal Hampshire Hospital standing directly opposite the entrance to the prison, and in 1964 the Remand Centre was built to house young offenders. It stayed in place until 1991 when it was used to house medium security 'Category C' adult males.

In 1995, after a period of sixty years as an all-male prison, the Annex began to house female prisoners. Renamed the West Hill Wing, it was used as a Democratic Therapeutic Unit. In the early twenty-first century the prison underwent a major refurbishment with a long-term build programme that included changes to make for safer custody and health care, along with a new electrical system, renewal of the fire and general alarms, a new visitor complex and pedestrian access at the main gate. A rebuild of C wing was completed in October 2008, but other plans for improvement were shelved due to financial reasons.

There have been a number of attempted escapes. In 1909, 30-year-old Belgian Johan Witer escaped after attacking a warder with an iron bar. He remained at liberty for four days as a massive manhunt took place across the region and, once detained, he was convicted of attempted murder and a further ten years added to his original sentence.

In December 2001, a convicted murderer managed to escape by scaling the wall and, using a homemade handsaw, he was able to saw through the bars of his ground-floor cell window. He then used a rope and grappling hook to scale the 30ft-perimeter wall. He was soon apprehended and returned to complete his sentence.

*

Like other gaols around the country, Winchester did not retain its own executioner. Instead, the under-sheriff of the local counties, in which the condemned prisoner had been sentenced to death, retained a copy of the short Home Office list of hangmen and assistants and selected an executioner from that, with the prison governor being responsible for recruiting the assistant executioner. Initially the hangman worked alone but by the turn of the century it became the norm to employ an assistant at all executions.

The first executions inside Winchester Gaol took place in the grounds adjacent to the plot of land where convicted murderers were buried. Following an incident at Exeter

To be submitted to the High Sheriff

Memorandum of Conditions to which any Person acting as Executioner is required to conform

1. An executioner is engaged and paid by the High Sheriff, and is required to conform with any instructions he may receive from or on behalf of the High Sheriff in connection with any execution for which he may be engaged.

2. A list of persons competent for the office of executioner is in the possession of High Sheriffs and Governors: it is therefore unnecessary for any person to make application for employment in connection with an execution, and such application will be regarded as objectionable conduct and may lead to the removal of the applicant's name from the list.

3. Any person engaged as an executioner will report himself at the prison at which an execution for which he has been engaged is to take place not later than 4 o'clock on the afternoon preceding the day of execution.

4. He is required to remain in the prison from the time of his arrival until the completion of the execution and until permission is given him to leave.

5. During the time he remains in the prison he will be provided with lodging and maintenance on an approved scale.

6. He should avoid attracting public attention in going to or from the prison; he should clearly understand that his conduct and general behaviour must be respectable and discreet, not only at the place and time of execution, but before and subsequently. In particular he must not reveal to any person, whether for publication or not, any information about his work as an Executioner or any information which may come his way in the course of his duty. If he does he will render himself liable to prosecution under the Official Secrets Acts 1911 and 1920.

7. His remuneration will be £10 ———— for the performance of the duty required of him, to which will be added £5 ———— if his conduct and behaviour have been satisfactory. The latter part of the fee will not be payable until a fortnight after the execution has taken place.

8. Record will be kept of his conduct and efficiency on each occasion of his being employed, and this record will be at the disposal of any High Sheriff who may have to engage an executioner.

9. The name of any person who does not give satisfaction, or whose conduct is in any way objectionable, so as to cast discredit on himself, either in connection with the duties or otherwise, will be removed from the list.

10. The apparatus approved for use at executions will be provided at the prison. No part of it may be removed from the prison, and no apparatus other than approved apparatus must be used in connection with any execution.

11. The executioner will give such information, or make such record of the occurrences as the Governor of the prison may require.

The Terms and Conditions that an executioner must adhere to. (Author's Collection)

Gaol, when there was a failed attempt to execute a prisoner on a badly constructed gallows, the government designed a new gallows and had blueprints made so all gallows would be constructed to a uniform design. They were also built undercover, initially in outbuildings such as stables and sheds housing the prison van, before a further modernisation saw gallows constructed indoors on a wing of the gaol utilising three cells for the scaffold. A first-floor cell was converted into a scaffold with the trapdoors forming the ceiling on the cell below, into which the condemned man would fall. The beams would be situated in the second-floor cell with chains hanging through holes cut in the floor onto which the noose would be attached in the first-floor cell.

The Home Office design for a new gallows. (Prison Service Museum)

William Calcraft officiated at the first private execution at Winchester. He had been a regular visitor to the city and had carried out executions outside the new gaol since it was opened in 1849. Calcraft was replaced by William Marwood, the pioneer of the long drop method which saw a humane approach to execution, with prisoners being given drops designed to break their necks rather than choke to death on the short drops Calcraft favoured using.

Marwood died in 1883 and was initially replaced by Bartholomew Binns, who carried out a number of botched executions across the country for several months until he was dismissed following a run-in with prison authorities. Binns was replaced by James Berry of Bradford, who visited the gaol on two occasions during his eight-year reign as the country's chief executioner.

Like Binns, Berry soon fell foul of the authorities and in 1891 he tendered his resignation, with his visit to the gaol in August of that year his last as a chief executioner in England. Berry was engaged to carry out one further execution in Scotland in January 1892 (which proved to be his last), and although he reapplied for the post on a number of occasions he had been replaced by a competent executioner, and his requests were ignored.

James Billington succeeded Berry as the country's chief executioner and made several visits to the prison in the latter years of the reign of Queen Victoria. Billington officiated at more executions at Winchester than any other hangman and carried out the last triple execution in Great Britain when he hanged three men at the gaol in July 1896. In the early twentieth century James's son, William, carried out two executions at the gaol, assisted on the second by his younger brother, John, who would also go on to become chief executioner.

In 1913, after almost a decade since the last execution at the gaol, John Ellis made his first visit to Winchester, for the execution of Augustus Penny. Although the LPC4 execution book (in which all data was recorded in relation to the execution) contains the details of his assistant, Albert Lumb, the assistant's details are crossed out and no comments are made in regards to his conduct. This would suggest that Lumb was engaged and reported for duty at the prison or cancelled at the very last minute, as his details were recorded in the book. Presumably Lumb became incapacitated and was unable to officiate. Similarly, in 1950, the details of hangman Stephen Wade are noted in the LPC4 book and crossed out, with another assistant's details written beneath it.

Ellis made four visits to the prison for the purpose of carrying out executions and, although there were no problems in the first two, on his next two visits the LPC4 book reports that the execution was not carried out successfully and the prisoner in both cases died of asphyxia rather than a broken neck.

As a result, an enquiry was held. In the report the prison's official inspector, rather that finding fault with Ellis's competency, praised his skill, stating that, 'He must now carry out his work in a fraction of a second.' According to the report, Ellis was concerned that the trapdoors of the gallows at the gaol were too narrow and the walk from the cell to the gallows was too long. The report found that the pit was almost 2ft narrower than the standard pit of 10ft 8in, such as the one at Pentonville, where in recent times 'more hangings have been carried out on this gallows than at any other in the kingdom.'

EXECUTIONS.—TABLE OF DROPS (OCTOBER, 1913).

The length of the drop may usually be calculated by dividing 1,000 foot-pounds by the weight of the culprit and his clothing in pounds, which will give the length of the drop in feet, but no drop should exceed 8 feet 6 inches. Thus a person weighing 150 pounds in his clothing will require a drop of 1,000 divided by 150 = 6⅔ feet, i.e., 6 feet 8 inches. The following table is calculated on this basis up to the weight of 200 pounds:—

TABLE OF DROPS.

Weight of the Prisoner in his Clothes.	Length of the Drop.		Weight of the Prisoner in his Clothes.	Length of the Drop.		Weight of the Prisoner in his Clothes.	Length of the Drop.	
lbs.	ft.	ins.	lbs.	ft.	ins.	lbs.	ft.	ins.
118 and under	8	6	138 and under	7	3	167 and under	6	0
119 ,,	8	5	140 ,,	7	2	169 ,,	5	11
120 ,,	8	4	141 ,,	7	1	171 ,,	5	10
121 ,,	8	3	143 ,,	7	0	174 ,,	5	9
122 ,,	8	2	145 ,,	6	11	176 ,,	5	8
124 ,,	8	1	146 ,,	6	10	179 ,,	5	7
125 ,,	8	0	148 ,,	6	9	182 ,,	5	6
126 ,,	7	11	150 ,,	6	8	185 ,,	5	5
128 ,,	7	10	152 ,,	6	7	188 ,,	5	4
129 ,,	7	9	154 ,,	6	6	190 ,,	5	3
130 ,,	7	8	156 ,,	6	5	194 ,,	5	2
132 ,,	7	7	158 ,,	6	4	197 ,,	5	1
133 ,,	7	6	160 ,,	6	3	200 ,,	5	0
135 ,,	7	5	162 ,,	6	2			
136 ,,	7	4	164 ,,	6	1			

When for any special reason, such as a diseased condition of the neck of the culprit, the Governor and Medical Officer think that there should be a departure from this table, they may inform the executioner, and advise him as to the length of the drop which should be given in that particular case.

Hangman's Table of Drops. (Author's Collection)

The execution chamber at Winchester would be identical to the one at Newgate. (Prison Service Museum)

The report concluded, 'I submit that the accidents in the two cases at Winchester were due to the opening being too narrow and I consider that a wider opening should be provided before another prisoner is hanged there.'

As a result, a new location for the gallows was found at Winchester and again it was located at the end of D wing near to the mortuary. The first man to be hanged in the new execution shed was Abraham Goldenberg. Two cells at the end of D wing were utilised to hold condemned prisoners and were directly linked to the execution chamber. The executioner and his assistant would enter through one door and the observers through the other and before an execution took place matting was placed on the floor so that the prisoners would not hear the footsteps of the execution party.

Prior to the purpose-built chamber, condemned prisoners were held in cells around the prison centre and had to walk down the spiral stairs and out to the shed in the area at the side of D wing. As this gallows was visible to prisoners at the side of D wing the inmates had to be moved out before an execution took place. Once the hospital was completed in 1908 the hangman and his assistant were billeted here, having previously been quartered in the old debtors' prison, which was inside the wall but was demolished during building work in the early 1900s.

Early in 1924 Ellis tendered his resignation and never returned to Winchester to see the new execution suite. He was succeeded by Tom Pierrepoint, who served as an executioner for over forty years. The gallows was used sparingly at Winchester during the mid-twentieth century and as a result Tom Pierrepoint would make a total of just four visits to the gaol. Probably the most famous of modern-day executioners, Albert Pierrepoint, nephew of Tom Pierrepoint, became a chief executioner in 1941, but didn't make his first visit to the gaol until 1949.

In 1894, William Rogers tried to commit suicide by cutting his throat. Although he suffered severe wounds to his neck, it was deemed safe to execute him and, although the wound tore open when the drop fell, the execution was carried out successfully.

In 1948 Pierrepoint had been appointed to carry out the execution at Winchester of William Gray, who had shot dead his wife at Hurn in Dorset. After killing his wife Gray shot himself in the jaw, injuring himself in such a way it was felt that he could not be hanged without risking either decapitation or strangulation, and as a result he was reprieved.

Also that year, Pierrepoint was engaged to hang James Camb at Winchester. Camb had been sentenced to death for the murder of Gay Gibson, a passenger on board the SS *Durban Castle* on which Camb was a steward. Despite no body being recovered, the prosecution's version of events – that Camb had thrown her body into the ocean through a porthole in her cabin – was believed by the jury and he was duly convicted. In Camb's case he was spared execution due to a temporary reprieve on all convicted murderers while the government debated whether to abolish the death penalty. William Gray and James Camb each served just eleven years and were released with a few months of each other in 1959.

On Albert Pierrepoint's second visit to Winchester, for a rare double execution, he took offence at the standard of the meal he and his assistants were served on the night before the execution. He raged when faced with a plate of ham and cress salad, despite it being a warm summer's evening, and demanded that the cook be brought back to rustle up something more substantial, or he would lead his men out on strike! Pierrepoint resigned in 1956 and was succeeded by Harry Allen, who had assisted Pierrepoint at the prison in 1949, and Les 'Jock' Stewart, who carried out the last two executions at the gaol.

Following the abolition of capital punishment in 1965, the execution chamber, or topping shed as the staff referred to it, was demolished to make way for an extension to the kitchen. The original burial ground of convicted prisoners was built over in the 1990s and as a result the bodies were exhumed and re-interred in a local cemetery.

A number of prison officers have mentioned that the area around the former execution chamber has a very strange atmosphere, especially at night. On night duty, staff are required to report in at certain points – pegs – during the night, and the pegging point at the far end of D1, by the drop, is said to be a particularly eerie place when on night duty. One officer said that, 'It is not a place to loiter in the early hours of the morning, in fact I know of a couple of big hard screws who won't go down there at night, I don't linger there myself when I'm on nights!'

Today, HMP Winchester continues as a Category B prison for adult males. This book looks in detail at the stories behind the thirty-one men who were all hanged at Winchester.

1

IN THE INTERESTS OF DISCIPLINE

William Dixon, 6 September 1869

Discipline has always been high on the requirements of the British Army and on occasions it can be harsh, sometimes even bordering on the brutal. In the summer of 1869, William Dixon, a 28-year-old private serving in the 7th Fusiliers, based at Aldershot, was having trouble with his corporal. A number of the soldiers, Dixon in particular, felt that the corporal inflicted unduly harsh treatment for even the tiniest indiscretion. The soldiers, five privates and a corporal, were billeted in Number 1 Hut, South Camp, and animosity between Dixon and the corporal, 30-year-old William Brett, stemmed from a number of reports issued against Dixon by Brett, a stickler for doing things 'by the book'. In the six months since January 1869, Brett had reported Dixon several times, for what had been termed trifling breaches of discipline. He had suffered a number of punishments for the offences but nothing more severe than being confined to barracks, the maximum for one offence being six days.

Matters came to a head on Tuesday afternoon, 22 July, when a number of men were detailed to fill mattresses with clean straw. All five privates billeted in the hut were tasked with the duty and three of them – Ben Adams, Robert Bunce and John Carter – were carrying out the work, while the other two, William Dixon and a soldier named Henshall, quickly tired of the laborious chore and went to the mess hall. Henshall was soon very drunk and began toying with his rifle, at one point even pointing it at another soldier in the mess. Word soon reached Cpls James Cross and William Brett about the soldiers' behaviour. They hurried to the canteen and ordered the men back to their hut. Cross then told Henshall he was going to be taken to the guardroom and held on a charge of being drunk on duty. Dixon pleaded with the corporals to be lenient on his comrade, but he was ignored and Henshall was placed under arrest.

Dixon was angered at the attitude of the higher-ranking men, Cpl Brett in particular, and when he saw through the window that Brett was heading back to the hut he picked up his service rifle and released the safety catch. Pte Adams saw what was happening and moved across to Dixon.

'For God's sake don't do that, Dixon!' he shouted, adding, 'Don't make a fool of yourself.' He then tried to disarm his comrade, only to be told, 'If you prevent me from doing what I am about to do you shall have it instead of him.'

Realising something dreadful was about to happen, Adams shouted at the corporals not to enter, but they either did not hear or chose to ignore the call, for moments later they reached the hut. As they passed through the doorway Dixon stepped out from behind the door and fired once, hitting Brett in the face and killing him instantly.

'You need not seize me,' Dixon said calmly. 'I know what I've done and I'm not sorry for it.'

Incidents of this kind were becoming commonplace and, as a result, the government decided that military murders should be tried as quickly as possible, to serve as a deterrent to unruly and recalcitrant soldiers. As there was no sitting of the assizes due in Hampshire, Dixon was sent for trial in London. He appeared before Mr Justice Montague Smith at the Old Bailey on Wednesday 18 August.

Dixon was described as a good-looking man, standing a little over 6ft tall, with a fine physique and military gait and with twelve years' service in the 7th Fusiliers, having served in Gibraltar, Malta and Canada. His counsel, Douglas Straight, offered a defence of insanity caused by drink. Unable to read and write, Dixon dictated a letter to his mother while he was on remand at Winchester Gaol in which he claimed he was sorry for what he had done but that the corporal was a tyrant who had deserved all he got.

The prosecution claimed it was simply a case of murder by a man who bore a grudge against another and there was no question of insanity, and that the prisoner had been sober when he fired the fatal shot and fully aware of his actions. The jury agreed and took only five minutes to find Dixon guilty as charged. Dixon was then housed in Newgate Gaol before being returned to Hampshire to face execution.

How the Illustrated Police News *recorded the murder of William Brett. (Author's Collection)*

Above left: *William Calcraft carried out the first private execution at Winchester. (Author's Collection)*

Above right: *The former prisoner's burial ground was also the site of the first gallows in the grounds of the gaol. (Alan Constable)*

On Monday 6 September he was hanged in the first private execution at Winchester Gaol. The gallows was erected in the grounds of the prison on the site where previously executed prisoners were buried. Beside the scaffold was a freshly dug grave with a pile of quicklime beside it. Shortly before 8 a.m. hangman William Calcraft pinioned the prisoner, who walked firmly as the grim procession made its way to the place of execution. Around fifty people waited outside the prison gates as Dixon was executed. As the drop fell a black flag was hoisted to show to the assembled crowd that justice had been done and William Brett had been avenged.

2

WITH SHAME AND SORROW

Thomas Smith, 16 November 1874

Had I not been drinking I should never have done such a deed …
Written confession by Tom Smith on the morning of his execution.

There were many similarities between William Dixon's crime and the offence that brought Pte Thomas Smith to the gallows, in the second private execution at Winchester. Smith had also shot dead a superior officer after being punished for a breach of discipline and, like Dixon, Smith was taken up to London to face trial at the Old Bailey; although they faced a different judge, both men were defended and prosecuted by the same counsel.

On the morning of Saturday 12 September 1874, members of 'D Troop' 20th Hussars based at Aldershot were taking part in musket practice. Under the command of Capt. John Dent Bird, the soldiers were using firing ranges at Cesar's Camp, a short distance from their base at West Cavalry Barracks. On arriving at the ranges at 9.30 a.m., the men split into two groups and began firing practice at a range of 250 yards. Each man fired five shots at this distance before moving to the next marker, 300 yards from the targets. Capt. Bird stood to one side of the flanks and gave the order for the next rounds to be fired. As the volleys rang out Capt. Bird was seen to slump to the ground. Initially it was thought that he had fainted, but when Sgt Tyrell Fairhead rushed to his side he found that Bird was bleeding from a wound to his chest.

He turned to look at the ranks and saw that 41-year-old Pte Smith was standing away from the rest of the men.

'Who did that?' the sergeant shouted and, noticing that Smith stood apart from the flanks and was still holding his rifle in the firing position, he asked him directly, 'Tom Smith, was that you who fired that shot?'

Smith made no attempt to deny his actions, declaring, 'I done it; who else do you think did it?' Throwing his carbine to the ground, Smith then removed his waist-belt and offered them to the sergeant as a gesture of surrender.

Capt. Bird died from his wounds ten minutes or so after being shot and later that morning Smith, after being placed under arrest and taken to the guardroom, was

Above: *How the* Illustrated Police News *recorded the murder of Captain Bird. (Author's Collection)*

Left: *The letter confirming that Thomas Smith had been executed. (Author's Collection)*

Below: *Hangman William Marwood. (Author's Collection)*

handed over to the officers from Hampshire Constabulary, who had the prisoner removed to Aldershot police station.

Capt. Bird, a 32-year-old widower with a young son at school in Germany, was a well-respected soldier, who had enlisted in 1869 and quickly risen up the ranks, becoming a captain in 1871. Smith, on the other hand, was a soldier with over sixteen years' experience and known as a man of bad character. While serving in India several years before, he had threatened to shoot a commanding officer and was sentenced to a long term of imprisonment in a military prison, and on the day prior to the shooting he had been reprimanded for falling out of ranks without permission. Smith was then charged with insubordination and confined to barracks for seven days.

As with Dixon five years before, Smith was taken from Hampshire to face trial at the Old Bailey and on Wednesday 28 October he appeared before Mr Justice Lush. Although Mr Straight, his defence counsel, tried to claim the shooting was an accident, Mr Harry Poland, for the prosecution, produced testimonies and witnesses supporting his view that there was provocation and that the shooting was the result of the punishment handed out to the prisoner on the day before the incident. The jury clearly believed the prosecution's version of events and needed just twenty minutes to bring in their verdict of guilty as charged.

While awaiting execution, Smith wrote a number of letters and admitted in one that 'Had I not been drinking I should never done such a deed.' In another he wrote: 'I own with shame and sorrow that I am guilty of the crime for which I am to die…'

As he was led to the gallows he confessed to the priest that, 'I know my neglect from my Bible and giving way to drink has brought me to this sad position'. As he reached the trapdoor he spoke one last time: 'in a few moments,' he claimed, 'Jesus Christ's arms will be open to receive me.'

He died without a struggle.

3

ALL DONE IN A MOMENT

James Caffyn, 11 February 1878

Shortly after dawn on Tuesday 27 November 1877, officers with the Portsmouth Police Force stationed at Portsea attended a morning briefing where they were furnished with a list of articles and issues to be dealt with that day. At the top of the agenda was a report of a man wanted for questioning over an incident across the Solent at Elmfield, near Ryde, on the Isle of Wight on the previous afternoon.

James Caffyn was described as being a 31-year-old illiterate dock labourer, just 5ft 2½ins tall, with a sallow complexion, sharp features and a sullen disposition. He had last been seen wearing dark trousers and a waistcoat, likely to be bloodstained.

Barely thirty minutes into his shift, PC James Thomas called into the Victoria Tavern, on Queen Street, Portsea, close to the dockyard gates. Despite the early hour – it was a little after 7 a.m. – the bar was doing a roaring trade and, surveying the morning drinkers, a motley collection of dockworkers, navvies and labourers, his attention was drawn to a man standing talking to a number of sailors. His dress matched that of the wanted man and, being short in height and visually like the description issued, Thomas approached and said, 'I believe you're the man, from your description, that I am looking for on a serious charge.'

Without turning around, the man calmly replied, 'I think you are mistaken, if ever a man was!'

'So much the best for you if I am,' PC Thomas told him. Adamant he was the man, and despite protestations to the contrary, the officer placed him under arrest and escorted him into custody.

At Portsea police station a witness who had travelled over from the Isle of Wight identified the prisoner as the wanted man and, later that day, after being charged with murder, he was taken by boat back to Ryde, where investigations were underway following the discovery of a brutal murder on the previous day.

At 5 p.m. that Monday afternoon, hawker John Barber had returned to his home at St Helen's, Elmfield, Ryde. Entering the front room, he had found the body of his daughter, 37-year-old Maria Barber, lying in the corner with her throat cut. There was only one suspect – Maria's boyfriend, James 'Jemmy' Caffyn – and the hunt for him quickly led to his arrest on the following morning.

At an inquest, held at the Lake Superior public house, Elmfield, on Wednesday 28 November, before coroner F. Blake esq., the story behind the murder of Maria Barber was told to the court. Taking the stand, John Barber said he lived in the house where the murder had taken place, with his 'missus' Caroline Brown, and he was the father of the dead girl. Maria, his daughter, had lived at the family home until she left the Isle of Wight in 1862. Barber hadn't seen his daughter again until October 1877, when she had unexpectedly turned up at the house in the company of a man she referred to as Jemmy. Maria told her father she had been living in Hastings when she met her brother, who had told her that her father had been asking after her. Hearing this, she quit the lodging house she was running and returned across the water.

Back on the island, she and Jemmy moved into her father's house, living as man and wife, and Caffyn quickly found labouring work at Brading Harbour. The couple appeared to be on good terms and everything seemed perfectly normal until Monday 26 November. That morning Caffyn did not leave to go to work as he usually did. Barber thought this odd but did not comment on it, and he left the house, with Caroline Brown, bidding goodbye to his daughter at 9 a.m.

Greengrocer Hugh Grist told the inquest that at 10.20 a.m. that Monday morning he was just coming out of his store when Maria, her clothes soaked in blood, came rushing towards him in a state of terror.

'For God's sake come in, he has kicked, punched and tried to strangle me!' she cried. Grist followed her back into the house, where he saw a half-dressed Caffyn standing near the door in a rage. As Grist approached the door Caffyn swore at Maria and demanded she go upstairs and get his clothes. Grist told the inquest he then heard Maria tell Caffyn that if he would leave the house she would give him all her money. Moments later Caffyn went upstairs and returned with a dog chain, telling Maria that if he left he would also be taking the small Maltese Terrier dog. Further arguments ensued and, although they were still quarrelling over the dog, Grist felt he wasn't needed any longer and left the house.

When Barber returned home later that afternoon he found the body of his daughter. Dr Alfred Woodward said that at 5.30 p.m. on Monday he was called to the house and found the body of Maria Barber with several cuts to her throat. Beside the body was a bloodstained axe.

Following his arrest in Portsmouth, Caffyn had been held in custody and made a number of statements admitting his guilt: 'I may as well tell you all about it. There will be no harm in telling you the truth as it will all be known,' he told detectives. Caffyn said that on the day of the murder he had not gone into work as normal but had gone into Ryde for a shave and a haircut. He added, 'When I came back she aggravated me and said she would leave me… I done the deed with an axe. It was all done in a moment.'

The inquest ended with Caffyn being remanded on a charge of wilful murder and, in due course, he appeared before Mr Justice Mellor at Winchester Assizes on Tuesday 22 January 1878. He pleaded not guilty.

The court heard that Maria Barber had married a man at Bognor in 1863, not long after she had moved out of the family home on the Isle of Wight. Her husband had soon left her as 'he could not put up with her ways anymore,' Caffyn had told detectives following his arrest.

With the prosecution's evidence based mainly on Caffyn's own confession that he had 'hit her three times with an axe', there was little doubt what the verdict would be. The prisoner went into the witness box and stated, 'If I had my will, no woman should be allowed to cohabit with a man, for it was the cause of all the murders in the country.' When asked to consider their verdict the jury didn't bother to even leave the box before finding Caffyn guilty as charged.

At Winchester Gaol Caffyn occupied number 2 condemned cell in the upper corridor of E wing. He remained firm and self-possessed while awaiting execution and, as the day neared, he grew more penitent and paid heed to the ministrations of the chaplain. On the morning of the execution he rose at 6.30 a.m. and ate a hearty breakfast. He was visited by the chaplain, who sat with him as the fatal hour approached.

At a few moments to eight, executioner Marwood entered the condemned cell and pinioned the prisoner's arms. Caffyn offered no resistance and made no comment as he was led into the corridor and the procession to the gallows formed. The route to the scaffold took them through a door at the end of the wing into the exercise yard where a scaffold had been constructed in the corner of the yard. A double row of steps led the prisoner onto the trapdoor and he climbed them with a firm step. On the scaffold Caffyn paused for second, surveying the beam with the rope hanging down, before he stepped briskly onto the trapdoors and lined his feet against the chalk mark Marwood had prepared.

After strapping the prisoner's ankles, the hangman placed the noose around Caffyn's neck and let the slack of the rope drape behind the prisoner's back. As the chaplain continued to recite prayers Marwood stepped back and pulled the lever. Caffyn dropped with a thud but did not die instantly; his hands and feet were seen to quiver convulsively for several seconds and death was not confirmed until several minutes later.

It was the last execution carried out in the open air at the prison.

4

ON THE HIGH SEAS

James Whelan, 31 May 1886

On 27 October 1885, James Whelan, a 22-year-old Irishman living in Windsor, Nova Scotia, signed on as a seaman aboard the Nova Scotian brigantine *Emma J. Shore*, sailing under a British flag from New York to the River Plate with a cargo of general merchandise. The vessel had a mixed crew but was comprised mainly of Scandinavians and Canadians. Five days into the voyage, second mate George Richardson found fault with Whelan's work and threatened to 'kick him out of the rigging.' He also warned Whelan to take care, as he would 'beat his brains out on a dark night'.

Whelan laughed off the threat and replied that if he saw Richardson again during the voyage he would kill him, stating in his strong Irish accent:

> I am going to take a solemn oath. If the second mate at any time takes a captain's bar or belaying pin to me, I am going to kill him dead at my feet, and the man who has half a word to say about it I shall shove my sheath knife through his heart. So help me God.

He then kissed a Bible.

For several days the men avoided seeing each other, but on the night of Sunday 15 November their paths crossed again. Whelan had been manning the wheel when, at 10 p.m., he was relieved from his post and moved to the rear of the vessel. Spying Richardson up ahead, Whelan picked up a 2ft long 2ins diameter belaying pin, used to secure the rigging. He walked quietly up behind him, smashed the pin down across his skull and then hurled him overboard. He then walked to the aft of the ship, pulled several times on the patent log line, used to measure the boat's speed, and cried out, 'Man overboard!'

A boat was launched, but no sign of the second mate was found. Two men who had witnessed the attack initially remained silent, fearful of the Irishman's threats and temper, but word soon reached the captain; on the following day Whelan's knife was taken from him and he was put in irons. Whelan admitted he had committed the murder, laughingly claiming that Richardson was now 'stoking coals for the Devil'. He

Mr Justice Day sentenced to death more murderers hanged at Winchester than any other judge. (T.J. Leech Archive)

was later taken to Buenos Aires and detained at the British Consul until a boat could take him back to England where, in due course, he landed at Southampton and was taken into custody charged with murder.

Whelan stood trial before Mr Justice Day at Winchester Assizes on 8 May. His defence was manslaughter through self-defence. Whelan claimed that he had been attacked by the second mate: in trying to save his own skin he had picked up the metal bar, and during the struggle Richardson had fallen overboard.

The prosecution's case was based on eyewitness testimony that the accused had yielded the fatal blow, plus evidence that he had sworn on the Bible he intended to kill the second mate. There was also the confession Whelan had made following his arrest. The jury agreed with this version of events.

Before he walked to the scaffold, Whelan left a note in his cell confessing to the murder of two other men on previous occasions.

5

THE MAIDEN VOYAGE

Albert Edward Brown, 31 May 1886

When the two-mast sailing ketch *Nellie* eased out of London's Millwall docks, on a coasting voyage with a cargo of seed, on Thursday 25 March 1886, the crew consisted of many experienced sailors and one young man making his first voyage. James Stanley Parker, an 18-year-old from Clapham, described by his own father as a delicate boy, soon found the motion of the vessel too much and spent four days confined to his quarters unable to do any work. He was helped out during his illness by another of the crew, 22-year-old Albert Brown, a native of Greenwich, who did many of the duties detailed for the sick man alongside his own.

The final destination of the *Nellie* was Southampton and they reached the port late on Saturday 3 April. The following days were taken up with unloading the cargo and the crew was discharged four days later on the Wednesday. Parker was paid 4s in wages, to add to the 5s he had brought with him, while the skilled waterman Brown collected 17s 6d. While on board the boat, Parker had loaned Brown 2s, which was returned when both were paid.

Once ashore, the crew headed straight for the public houses of Southampton and, in the early hours of the following morning, they then set off to tramp back to London, despite the weather being wet and stormy. Brown had now spent most of his money on drink, but his young companion had been more cautious with what he spent and what he drank. Reaching the city of Winchester, Parker and Brown were last seen together in the vicinity of Worthy Road at Barton Hill. Brown was later observed alone at the railway station where he boarded a train to London.

At 4 p.m. on the Friday afternoon, Henry Piper was working on a farm when he was asked to fetch a seed drill. Making his way across to the field, he noticed one of the hayricks had been disturbed and straw was scattered about. As he approached, he saw that some of the straw was covered in what looked like blood. He then realised that it had been used to cover the body of a man. He called for help and blacksmith Alf Taylor rushed to his side. Taylor confirmed that there was indeed a body covered in straw and together they summoned police officers from nearby Easton. At 5.30 p.m. PCs Gladwell and Smith arrived at the scene. They found it was the body of a young man and that his throat had been cut so severely he had almost been decapitated.

The body was soon identified as that of the James Parker, and Brown was quickly traced to Greenwich and when arrested police found bloodstains on his clothing. He was brought to Winchester to face charges. Meanwhile, a post-mortem carried out by a Dr Richards found that the young man had sustained a number of wounds to the head, consistent with having been made with a hammer, and his throat had been cut down to the spine. The skipper of the *Nellie*, Frank Roberts, told detectives that when Brown was discharged from the ketch he was carrying a hammer, chisel, gimlet and sheaf knife in his bag.

Brown stood trial before Mr Justice Day at Winchester Assizes on Monday 11 May. His defence was that he was not the man who had committed the murder and it was a case of wrongful identification by the witnesses. The prosecution put forward a strong case based on witness testimony and bloodstains on the prisoner when arrested. The prosecution also found that Brown had promised his wife he would return home with 10s and when he had returned to Greenwich he had handed over the money. This was despite members of the crew testifying that he had spent most of his wages on drink.

The trial went into a second day and the jury needed over an hour before returning their verdict of guilty as charged. Once sentence of death had been passed on him, Brown admitted that he had killed his colleague by hitting him with a hammer and then cutting his throat with a razor. The motive was to rob Parker of the 4s wages he was carrying.

Brown was hanged beside Whelan (see chapter 4) in the first double execution at the gaol. Since the previous execution at Winchester, eight years before, when Caffyn was hanged in the prison yard, the Home Office had designed a new gallows. In the previous year an execution had caused controversy at Exeter when a gallows constructed by the prison carpenter had failed to operate: the trapdoor refused to open when the hangman pulled the lever. When the doors failed to open a second time the prisoner was taken back to his cell and the scaffold inspected; a reprieve was ordered and an investigation carried out. It found that the carpenter had used a thinner wood that normal; as the scaffold had been left standing in the open in the prison yard (during which time it had rained incessantly) the wood had swollen to the extent that, when the weight of a man was placed on it, the faces of the trapdoors butted together tightly and would not open.

To prevent this from happening again, it was decided to erect scaffolds indoors in sheds or in prison wings and the apparatus was built to a template designed by Home Office engineers. At Winchester the gallows was erected in the centre of the shed used to store the prison van. It had an asphalt floor with a deep pit constructed beneath, onto which two large wooden trapdoors were placed; they were secured by a three-lever bolt which, when withdrawn, released the doors. At either side, at a height of 7ft, holes had been cut into the wall, and the beam from which the rope was suspended was inserted into these holes.

Hangman James Berry of Bradford had been on duty that morning at Exeter and it was he who was engaged at Winchester for the double execution.

On the morning of the execution both prisoners breakfasted well and confessed to the chaplain before they walked, without any signs of fear, to the scaffold. Whelan, the

Hangman James Berry made just two trips to Winchester to carry out executions. (Author's Collection)

heavier of the two, was given a drop of just 4ft, while Brown was given a drop of 6ft 6ins. 'Lord Jesus receive my soul,' Brown called out as the noose was placed around his neck.

Dr Richards, who had carried out the post-mortem on Brown's victim, examined both men once the trapdoors had crashed open, and found that, in the case of Brown, there was no dislocation of the neck. There was violent inspiration for four minutes, and his face showed signs of suffering. He found that Brown's pulse continued to beat for 12½mins. Brown had weighed 10 stone at execution.

In the case of Whelan, who tipped the scales at 13 stone, his death appeared instant as there were no signs of any pain or suffering. His pulse also beat for ten minutes and the diaphragm beat for three minutes. This information was later used in the Aberdare Report set up to investigate the working practices and competence of the executioners.

6

UNCOMMON AFFECTION

George Clarke, 27 March 1888

Hereford-born George Clarke had held a variety of jobs before becoming the landlord of the Prince Albert Inn at Newtown, Aldershot. A tailor by trade, he then signed up to the army, serving twenty-two years in the 36th Regiment and 1st Leicestershire Regiment. On his retirement in June 1886, having earned good conduct and long service medals, he received a pension and began working as a boot repairer in a shop next door to the Prince Albert, and when the tenancy came up for the public house in the following September, he became the landlord. Forty-two-year-old Clarke ran the public house with his wife of fifteen years, and also living on the premises were their five children: two from one of Mrs Clarke's previous marriages and three from this union.

No sooner had Clarke taken over running the inn than quarrels broke out between husband and wife due to his relationship with his stepdaughter, Annie Vaughan. It seems Clarke and Annie had had an affair but had stopped when his wife, her mother, began to suspect something was going on.

Annie Vaughan was described as being very prepossessing and had no shortage of admirers from customers in the bar. In January 1888 she began a relationship with Charles Clarke (no relation), a private in the Medical Staff Corp based at a nearby camp and, although her stepfather initially objected to it, especially as her suitor was of a lowly rank, he gradually came around and accepted it.

However, by the end of that month relations between husband and wife had deteriorated to the extent that she took the children and moved into lodgings. On Saturday 4 February Clarke paid her a visit and persuaded his wife to come home. Mrs Clarke and four of the children came back that day but Annie, now 18 years old, didn't return until the following night.

On Monday morning one of the children saw Clarke leaving the bedroom, which they all shared. When another of the children tried to rouse their sister, she was found lying in a pool of blood. Their screams brought Mrs Clarke rushing to the bedroom, passing Clarke who was standing in the passage in his shirt and underwear clutching a bloodstained razor.

THE ALDERSHOT MURDER.

EXECUTION AT WINCHESTER

At eight o'clock on Tuesday, within the precincts of the grim old prison at Winchester, George Clarke, the Aldershot murderer, satisfied with his life the demands of earthly law and justice. Notwithstanding all that has been said and written about the expediency of abolishing capital punishment in this country, it must be admitted that so long as our code of criminal jurisprudence requires "a life for a life," the case of the wretched man who was on Tuesday hurled into eternity was one which called for the strict enforcement of the dread penalty which is now and has been for some years past reserved for criminals convicted of wilful murder. The circumstances surrounding and immediately leading up to the crime for which Clarke was condemned to suffer death were of the most sickening and revolting character, while the murder itself was committed with a cold-blooded deliberation and determination of purpose which left not a vestige of hope that any efforts put forth on behalf of the convict would secure "any interference with the due course of law." That his doom was certain was made clear to him by the Judge before whom the case was tried on Tuesday, the 6th inst., and no attempt whatever was made to secure a commutation of the sentence on the hollow plea of "temporary insanity" set up by his counsel at the trial. Abandoning all hope of mercy, the culprit, from the moment he left the dock of the Assize Court and entered the gloomy condemned cell of one of the gloomiest prisons in the kingdom, gave himself up entirely to the ministrations of the Chaplain, the Rev. J. A. Ladbrooke, in preparing to appear before that Supreme Judge to whom he has still to answer for his misdeeds, in spite of the terrible ordeal through which he was on Tuesday called upon to pass.

A newspaper report of the execution of George Clarke. (Author's Collection)

'You've murdered my child!' Mrs Clarke screamed at her husband, who calmly replied, 'Yes, I did it.' Clarke then went downstairs into the bar and, after picking up a bottle of spirits, bade goodbye to the terrified children, who huddled in the lounge, and fled out of the door.

The police and a doctor were summoned and it was found that Annie's throat had been cut so savagely that her head was almost severed. In the meantime a hunt for the killer began, and within a short time Edward Heddrington, licensee of the Heroes of Lucknow public house, having heard of the murder, set out in pursuit of Clarke on horseback and detained him at nearby Ash Church until a PC Gough was able to place him under arrest.

At his Winchester Assizes trial, before Mr Justice Field, the court heard that there had been intimacy between the prisoner and his young stepdaughter for two years and he had become jealous of her relationship with the young soldier. His 11-year-old son James and 13-year-old daughter Lily both gave evidence at the trial and in tears they said that their father had entered the room shortly before their sister was discovered dead in her bed.

Although Clarke offered a defence of temporary insanity, the jury had no hesitation in finding him guilty as charged when asked to consider their verdict and, passing sentence, Mr Justice Field said that in twelve years he had never heard as sad and shocking a case.

7

ALL TO DO WITH DRINK

Esther Emily Watts had known tragedy. During her fourteen years of marriage she had given birth to seven children, only to watch them die in infancy one by one, with just one child surviving. Despite the heartache, she tried to live a happy life, doting on her son, but relations with her husband were deteriorating so rapidly that, in the spring of 1891, 32-year-old Esther left their home in London and, taking their 5-year-old son, went to live with her father in Jubilee Terrace, in the Portsea area of Portsmouth. Here she found work at the nearby Brunswick laundry and set about trying to rebuild her life.

Her husband, 38-year-old Henry Watts, had for several years served in the Royal Militia out in India before he was discharged after suffering sunstroke. Returning home, he had then joined the Royal Navy serving five years as an able seaman until he was invalided out in the summer of 1887. In the following four years his dependence on alcohol, along with a growing inclination not to work, eventually became too much for Esther to cope with. When sober, his behaviour was exemplary and he was a loving husband and father, but when in drink he was quarrelsome and irritating in his manner and on several occasions he had resorted to violence. It was to be a violent attack on his wife, again while drunk, that caused her to pack her bags and leave.

On Friday 4 April, Watts left London and travelled to Portsmouth and, learning that his wife was at work, he waited outside the laundry until she finished for the day at 8 p.m. They chatted briefly and passers-by heard raised voices and what sounded like threats being issued by Watts. They parted and Watts headed for the Derby Tavern on Derby Road, where, after downing three pints of ale in quick succession, he asked the landlord for a pencil and paper. He then wrote out a note, which he folded and placed in his pocket.

Shortly before 4 p.m. on the following afternoon, a drunken Watts turned up at Jubilee Terrace, asking to see his wife. The door was opened by Esther's younger brother, 15-year-old William Hinkley. Watts was shown into the rear parlour where Esther was sitting nursing their son, who was suffering with the measles. Also in the room was her father, George Hinkley, and when Watts asked to speak to his wife alone, Esther told

SHOCKING MURDER AT STAMSHAW

A WOMAN SHOT BY HER HUSBAND.

ATTEMPTED SUICIDE OF THE MURDERER.

Disaster has followed disaster at Portsmouth. Hardly had the public excitement cooled down from fever heat concerning the fatal fire in Commercial-road, on the 28th ult., when, on Saturday evening last, just a week later, Portsmouth was horrified by the news of a wife murder at Stamshaw. Inquiries proved that the rumour was only too well founded. The terrible occurrence took place at Jubilee House, Twyford-avenue, where, in the presence of her younger brother, a lad of fifteen, and her only surviving child, a boy of five, Esther Watts was shot dead by her husband. Afterwards the wretched man attempted to commit suicide with the same revolver, but only succeeded in inflicting a wound in his wrist. Watts was taken into custody soon afterwards, and conveyed to the Buckland Police-station, whence he was conveyed to the Police-court on Monday morning and charged with the murder at the ordinary sitting of the Magistrates.

him, 'What you have to say, you can say before father.'

Deciding on discretion, George Hinkley left the couple and their son alone in the room and went into the back garden, only to rush back inside when he heard what sounded like fierce quarrelling followed by gunshots. Hinkley entered the room and found his daughter slumped in a chair with blood streaming from fatal gunshot wounds to her throat and chest. Watts had then turned the gun on himself, only for the bullet to enter his wrist, passing clean through and missing the vital arteries. His son, on a sofa across the room, had witnessed everything. Hinkley's other son-in-law, William Lancaster, who was at the house at the time, also rushed into the room and managed to push Watts away as he went to retrieve the gun, which Hinkley then picked up and refused to hand back to the drunken killer.

'It's no use sending for a policeman,' Watts cried, 'she's dead and I'll be dead before a policeman gets here.'

Ignoring this, William Hinkley rushed from the house and quickly returned with PC Stephen Darcy, who had been on duty at Kingston Cross. Watts was placed under arrest and told the constable as he was led away, 'She was too good for me, she would never have lived with me and I could not have asked her to forgive me.' He was then taken to Buckland police station and remanded in custody, pending trial.

Edward Watts pictured in the press.
(Author's Collection)

Mrs Esther Watts.
(Author's Collection)

Watts pleaded not guilty to the charge of wilful murder when he appeared before Mr Justice Cave at Winchester Assizes on Monday 3 August. Despite it being a Bank Holiday the court was packed as they heard how Esther Watts had fled her home in London's New Cross district on 16 March after her husband, while drunk, had tried to strangle her. Watts had then written numerous letters to his wife, all of which went unanswered and, on the day before he travelled south, he had purchased a revolver from a pawnbroker.

His defence counsel vainly tried to show he was insane, citing the sunstroke he had contracted in India as proof, but the prosecution were able to convince the jury that the fact he had purchased the gun on the afternoon prior to the murder was proof that the murder was premeditated, and the jury needed just twenty-five minutes to find him guilty as charged.

He was hanged by James Berry, carrying out his last execution in England.

8

OVER A TRIFLING MILITARY OFFENCE

George Mason, 6 December 1893

As far as military punishments went it wasn't the most severe, but for 19-year-old George Mason it was enough to drive him to murder. Mason, a former costermonger, sometimes known as George Beckworth, had enlisted in the 3rd Battalion of the East Surrey Regiment, stationed at Fort Widley, Portsdown Hill, Portsmouth. On 26 June 1893, Mason was reported by the sergeant of his company, James Robinson, for refusing an order to return a number of mess tins from the shooting range back to the kitchens. Brought up in front of a tribunal, he was found guilty of the offence and sentenced to be confined to barracks for three days.

On the following day, while taking part in rifle practice on ranges at Port Creek, Hillsea, Mason pointed the gun at Sgt Robinson and shouted, 'Here's a good mark!' Pte Pope, standing beside Mason, told him to put down his rifle, but instead he carefully took aim and fired, stating coldly, 'Now I am level with him, he ran me in yesterday, now I have run him in!' The sergeant was hit once in the back and fell down dead.

Taken into custody, Mason showed no remorse for his actions, claiming that if it hadn't been for another soldier, Pte Jim Hearn, he would have 'Popped off Colour-Sergeant Reynolds as well!' He was also alleged to have told the arresting officer that he would be dancing a hornpipe in the air one of these days or face twenty years on account of his age.

His defence at Winchester Assizes, where he appeared before the fearsome Mr Justice Hawkins, was based on hereditary insanity. The defence produced two doctors to support this claim, along with the boy's uncle who told the court that several members of the family were housed in an asylum. The prosecution claimed it was simply a premeditated attack by a soldier who bore a grudge against a superior. They pointed to the confession Mason had made after being placed under arrest: he had told a military policemen, 'I shot him in the back and I meant to kill him.'

The jury needed just a short time to find him guilty as charged and, despite his age, he went to the gallows on a cold winter morning six months after committing a brutal murder.

George Mason's crime as featured in the Illustrated Police News. *(Author's Collection)*

Hangman James Billington carried out more executions at Winchester than any other modern-day hangman. (Author's Collection)

9

REVENGE

There were gasps of shock and surprise in the packed courtroom when the clerk asked the prisoner how he pleaded. In a barely audible voice he replied, 'Guilty.' Mr Justice Lawrence looked down from the bench and then at both counsels, before addressing the prisoner.

'Do you know the seriousness of the charge you have pleaded guilty to? Do you know what my duty will be?'

'Yes,' the prisoner replied, regaining his composure, 'you will sentence me to death.'

The prisoner, 45-year-old Samuel Elkins, had been charged with the murder of 54-year-old William Mitchell at Christchurch, Bournemouth. Mitchell, the father of ten children, many grown up, had been the tram-yard manager of the Bournemouth, Boscombe and Westbourne Omnibus Co. at Pokesdown for the last two years. Samuel Elkins, known at work as Tom, had been employed at the yard for over four years and his duties included preparing fodder for the horses and driving the gas engine and chaff-cutting machine. Elkins did not get on well with Mitchell, who seemed to be always looking for fault in his work, and in February 1894 he found cause to dismiss him on a charge of dishonesty and assaulting one of the apprentices at the yard. Elkins was given a week's pay in lieu and told to leave at once. 'That's this week's money, that's next week's money, and that's the end of you!' Mitchell told him.

Elkins was enraged and stormed round to the home of William Mate, chairman of the Board of Directors for the omnibus company. Elkins was told by the chairman that there was nothing he could do as Mitchell was in charge of the running of the yard.

'What shall I do? I have a wife and three children depending on me and I do not know where to look for another job!'

Although sympathetic, Mate told Elkins he was unable to help, but he promised to speak to Mitchell at the first opportunity, and advised him to do the same to see if he could change his mind. Elkins made some remarks about Mitchell's son, which Mate did not understand, before storming off. He was upset but did not appear to be threatening nor give any indication of the dreadful events that were about to happen.

On Monday morning, 22 February, Elkins visited a gun shop on Southampton's High Street, telling the salesman that he wanted a revolver to shoot a horse. The salesman suggested a rifle, but Elkins said he wanted something to carry in his pocket and purchased a large-bore revolver and twelve cartridges, paying £1 for them, and then returning to Bournemouth.

Later that afternoon he went to the tram yard only to be told that Mitchell was not on site. He told one of his former workmates, 'I daresay someone will wonder what I am waiting for. It's a long lane that has no turning, but there might be a turning now!'

The following morning Elkins returned to the yard and learned that Michell was tending to a horse. Elkins entered the stables, pulled out the revolver and fired at Mitchell, fatally wounding him. The gunshots brought other workers rushing to the stable, by which time Elkins had slipped away and headed for the town centre.

At 10.30 a.m. he approached Police Sergeant Robin Hood, stationed at Boscombe, who was on duty in Christchurch Road.

'Sergeant, will you have a drink with me?' Elkins asked him.

'No, I'm a tee-totaller,' the policeman told him.

'I must give myself up to you,' Elkins told him, and when asked why, he said, 'come and have a drink with me and I'll tell you!'

Sergeant Hood said he had not received any report on Elkins, to which he replied, 'If you wait here while I go get a drink, I'll tell you,' before entering the Palmerston Hotel. Hood waited outside and was soon rejoined by Elkins. Hood asked him why he wanted to give himself up and was told, 'I've done the crime, and had my revenge, and now I must suffer the law. I shot Mitchell up at Pokesdown this morning.' He then handed Hood the revolver telling him to be careful as it was still loaded.

Taken to the police station, Elkins told how he had visited the chairman and he was advised to try to get Mitchell to change his mind. He said that he had taken a train to Southampton, bought a revolver and then gone to the tram yard where he confronted Mitchell.

'I told him that if he didn't come to terms with me I would come to terms with him, and I up with the revolver and fired it off. It struck him here,' said Elkins, putting his hand to the back of his head, 'and he fell down dead.'

Elkins' trial took place at Hampshire Assizes on Monday 25 June and, with the guilty plea, it was a simple matter of sentence of death being passed in a trial lasting a matter of minutes. A date of execution was set for three clear Sundays from the date of sentence and Elkins duly walked calmly to the gallows.

10

MURDER AT THE CRICKETERS ARMS

Cyrus Knight, 12 December 1894

The Cricketers Arms, a small roadside inn situated on the main highway between Binsted and Blacknest, near Alton, was being looked after by 45-year-old Cyrus Knight and his wife Frances, eight years his junior. The couple were helping out the landlord, Frances' 93-year-old father, Complin Honeybourne, who was now frail and infirm, and they shared their quarters at the Cricketers Arms with their adopted son, 15-year-old William Lucas Brewer.

Well known locally for his violent temper, Knight, a former carter, had already been in court in 1883 when he was charged alongside two other men, one of them his brother, having been implicated in the shooting dead of one Henry Carter a few days before Christmas in the previous year. Knight and his brother were acquitted, while the third man, Andrew Fullick, was sentenced to eight months imprisonment at Winchester Gaol.

Relations between Knight and his wife, widowed from a previous marriage, were often strained and they lived unhappily together. On Friday evening, 28 September 1894, Knight was in the public bar playing a game of dominoes with a man named Sampson Light, a hop-picker who was residing at the inn while working in the area. At 7.30 p.m. Frances came into the bar and told her husband that his tea was ready. When there was no reply she approached and asked if they were nearly done with the game.

'As soon as this game is over I'll come,' Knight told her, finally leaving his seat fifteen minutes after being called. As he sat down to his meal, Frances chastised him for spending much of the afternoon drinking both in their own bar and in the various public houses around town. Knight reached for the milk jug and poured some into his teacup – and then he suddenly picked up the cup and threw it in his wife's face.

As the liquid dripped down her face and onto her breast she picked up her cup, containing hot tea, and returned the gesture. Knight then jumped to his feet, put on his overcoat, and went into an adjoining room, shouting, 'You shall not throw any more tea at me!'

Moments later he returned to the kitchen with a double-barrelled, breech-loading gun and, pointing it through the partly opened door, fired two shots at his wife. One entered her left jaw, the other her neck, and she fell to the ground without saying a word. William Brewer rushed into the bar shouting for help as Knight fled from the inn, heading towards Cobbetts Copse, a nearby wood.

Knight spent the night away from the inn before deciding to return on the following morning and face the consequences. Police officers had already been searching for him; they had been informed of the murder and had set up a manhunt.

As he approached the Cricketers Knight was spotted and detained. Inspector Hawkins of Hampshire Constabulary, based in Alton, told Knight he was under arrest for the murder of his wife. 'I could not help it,' he said, claiming that the gun had gone off after he caught it against the doorframe, adding, 'I am sorry, it was an accident.'

Knight stood trial before Mr Justice Grantham on Saturday 17 November at Winchester Assizes, standing in the same dock he had stood in a decade or so previously. The prosecution stated that this was a premeditated crime committed in anger after the victim had cursed and assaulted the accused.

His defence was that the shooting was accidental and that he had not intended to kill his wife. Sampson Light told the court that he had given the gun to Knight a couple of days before as he was hoping to sell it and a gunsmith who examined the murder weapon claimed that it had a heavy pull, and, as such, it was unlikely to have gone off accidentally and would have needed significant force on the trigger to make it fire.

The jury needed just ten minutes to reach a verdict and this time he was convicted and sentenced to death. The jury added a strong recommendation for mercy, but having considered the jury's comments, the Home Secretary refused application for a reprieve, stating the law must take its course.

11

THE STRONGEST AND MOST DANGEROUS MOTIVE

William Rogers, 12 December 1894

In April 1894, 51-year-old dockworker and former sailor William Rogers appeared before magistrates in Southampton charged with an assault on cab driver Charles Jupe. The victim of the attack was the husband of 34-year-old Sarah Jupe and Rogers had called at Jupe's house at 27 Northam Street and knocked him out of his chair – which he then used to strike the man as he lay on the floor. Rogers had previously lodged with the Jupes, but when he began to pay too much attention to Sarah her husband threw him out. Sarah had, it seem, moved out and gone to stay with Rogers for a time before deciding to return to her husband. In a jealous rage, Rogers had gone back to the house and made the assault, which was to earn him two months imprisonment.

Prison didn't seem to have taught Rogers anything, for no sooner was he back in Southampton than he began to pester Sarah Jupe. While she might have had some affection for Rogers at one time, she now felt none, and, while she was happy to chat and share a drink with him, she had no inclination to rekindle their romance.

Rogers had spent most of his life at sea and had no family, nor had he married, and as Sarah Jupe was the first person who had treated him with any real affection he found it hard to let her go. If she had considered the situation Sarah Jupe might have taken steps to avoid any run-ins with Rogers, but she was far too fond of drink to have any such feelings and their paths often crossed in pubs and clubs across the city. They saw each other several times during that summer of 1894, and the more he saw her the more he tried to renew their romance. Whether she encouraged him or led him on isn't clear, but it seems they began to have a number of quarrels in public, usually when they were both drunk. This culminated over the August Bank Holiday when he made threats to kill her.

On 24 September, Rogers spent the afternoon drinking in a number of public houses around the city, finishing the evening in the Pure Drop Inn at Kingsland. At 9.30 p.m. Mrs Jupe, in the company of her lodger Elie Le Fouvre, entered and made for the bar where they ordered drinks. Both Sarah and Elie had already consumed a number of drinks before reaching the Pure Drop Inn. Rogers, who lodged a few doors from the inn on Broad Street, was standing at the bar when the women entered and asked Sarah to join him in a drink. She refused, telling him she had just purchased one.

A short time later, seeing her glass was empty, he again offered to buy her a drink, but instead of accepting she reached forward, tipped some of his drink into her glass and walked off laughing. Rogers turned away and sat down across the room. When she later began dancing and singing in the bar Rogers approached purposely and put his arm around her neck as if to kiss her. Instead, he suddenly pulled out a razor and drew it across her throat, killing her instantly. Realising what he had done, he turned the razor on himself, causing a terrible gash to his own throat. He then slumped to the ground and lapsed into unconsciousness.

The police were summoned. Police Sergeant Strange found that the woman had died from her wounds, but that Rogers was still breathing. With help from a number of customers he was able to stem the bleeding and ferry the murderer to hospital.

Rogers recovered sufficiently to stand trial and appeared before Mr Justice Grantham at Winchester Assizes on Monday 19 November. Mr Bernard Coleridge QC, leading for the prosecution, claimed that it was a brutal crime committed through jealousy, calling it 'the strongest and most dangerous motive'. The defence tried to claim that the prisoner had been insane at the time of the murder, but it was a hopeless case – and the prisoner had already resigned himself to the outcome.

After the judge's summing up, it took the jury just thirty seconds to agree on a verdict and, without even leaving their seats, they found Rogers guilty of murder.

With no relatives, Rogers had just one visitor as he awaited the hangman, his landlady, to whom he bequeathed all his worldly goods at a farewell interview.

He was hanged alongside Cyrus Knight by James Billington. It had been a busy week for the Bolton hangman, who had travelled down from Newcastle where he had been engaged on the previous day, having already officiated at Leicester on the Monday. Billington arrived at Winchester in good time on the Tuesday evening, despite worries before that the bad weather would mean he would be delayed. At the prison he met up with his assistant, William Wilkinson. William had travelled directly from Bolton, having not been needed for the two previous executions as just one man had been hanged in each.

On the morning of the execution both prisoners were moved to adjacent cells in the basement of the prison so as to be closer to the gallows. On the stroke of eight the hangmen entered the cells, Billington pinioning Knight while Wilkinson went to secure Rogers. As the procession was formed, Rogers kicked off his shoes and declared, 'That's better. I'll not die in those. It was them that brought me here!'

The prisoners were on the scaffold in seconds and quickly dispatched. Both died instantly, although in the case of Rogers the self-inflicted wound to his neck was torn open, spraying blood around the pit.

12

TO BE FREE FROM RESPONSIBILITY

Philip Matthews, 21 July 1896

Early on the morning of Tuesday 7 April 1896, the body of a child was found in a field at Baffin's Farm, Copney, on the outskirts of Portsmouth. The young girl was smartly dressed and lying on her back under a bush with her head resting on a neatly folded bundle of child's clothes. The police were quickly summoned and the surgeon, Dr Lysander Maybury, was soon able to tell them that, although the girl had been manually strangled, there was no evidence of any sexual assault. There was nothing to help police identify the young girl and it was over forty-eight hours before they learned that she was 6-year-old Elsie Gertrude Matthews, the daughter of a Philip Matthews.

Matthews, a twice-married 32-year-old widower, was employed as a coachman to a Dr Piggott at Teignmouth, Devon. Elsie had been the illegitimate child of his first wife, Elizabeth, and when she died in 1892, while Elsie was still a baby, Matthews looked after her as if she was his own. His second marriage, to Maria, took place that August, but wasn't a happy one; on one occasion Matthews had discussed separation and told her he wanted to put Elsie in the care of the local union workhouse. She refused. Perhaps if she had accepted that their relationship was doomed and agreed to her husband's suggestion to have the child cared for it would have saved two lives. But it was not to be.

In the autumn of 1895, Matthews met Charlotte Mahoney, a very attractive single woman who wore fashionable clothes, gold-rimmed glasses, and had long, flowing dark hair. Originally from Kingston, Portsmouth, she was working in Teignmouth as a parlour maid.

Although Charlotte knew of Matthews' previous marriages, he had not been truthful about the state of his current relationship. Believing him to be legally parted from his second wife, Charlotte (who had just discovered that she was pregnant) accepted his offer of marriage. They had decided to visit her parents over the Easter weekend and make plans for their wedding.

On Good Friday Matthews handed in his notice at work and on the following morning he and Charlotte left Teignmouth separately and made for Exeter, from where they travelled to Portsmouth. There he was introduced to her family as her future husband. While maintaining the façade of being a happy bridegroom-to-be, Matthews was keeping a troubling secret to himself: far from being divorced, Matthews had been living in lodgings with Maria and the young child on Teign Street, Teignmouth. When he told her he was planning to marry Charlotte Mahoney she declared that she would no longer look after Elsie – he would have to care for her himself. She told him he had better sort out the situation by the end of the Easter weekend or she would 'make trouble for him'.

He was then faced with a problem. Charlotte would accept him having two past marriages, but he knew she would certainly not want to take care of another woman's child as they began married life together, especially as they had not discussed this while making their plans.

On Easter Sunday Matthews left Portsmouth, telling Charlotte he had some affairs to tie up regarding their impending marriage, which was to take place at Salisbury, and that he would return on the following day. He returned to Teignmouth and spent the night at the lodgings he shared with his wife, leaving in the morning in the company of the young child. The landlord, Joseph Wescott, having heard sounds of them quarrelling, told Matthews as he left the house with the child that if he caused Elsie any harm he would come looking for him.

The child's body was found on the Tuesday morning and when reports of the discovery reached the papers landlord Wescott contacted the police and later identified the body as that of Elsie Matthews. A hunt was set up for Matthews, who was eventually traced to Fareham after he telegraphed his employer, Dr Piggott, to ask that he send some money owed in wages. Detectives called at The Lamb, where Matthews and his paramour were staying, and placed him under arrest.

When he appeared before Mr Justice Day on Friday 26 June the prosecution claimed that he had committed a dreadful murder in order to be free from the responsibility of the young child. Although there was a lot of public interest in the case, with many believing that Charlotte had induced him to carry out the murder, it was shown in court that she was entirely unaware of the crime, nor had she any knowledge that the child was illegitimate and not the result of Matthews' marriage to his second wife.

The defence claimed that Matthews had accidentally strangled the child as they had slept under the hedge after making their way to Portsmouth from Teignmouth. Realising what he had done, they explained, he had panicked. Fearing that he would not be believed if he told the truth (that Elsie's death had been an accident), he decided to act as though nothing had happened.

The prosecution claimed that there was nothing to show that the prisoner was insane, and that the defence of an accident was clearly untrue; the jury needed just seventeen minutes, when debating their verdict, to agree.

13

THE SOUTHAMPTON CUT-THROAT MURDER

Frederick Burden, 21 July 1896

On Thursday afternoon, 20 February 1896, the body of Lena Faithfull was found in her bedroom at her lodgings at 9 Brooklyn Road, Portswood, Southampton. A young girl who ran errands for Mrs Faithfull called at the house at 1 p.m. and found the woman lying in a pool of blood in bed. She hurried home to tell her father – who in turn contacted the police.

Inspector Hurst, from the Hampshire Constabulary, based in Southampton, called at the house. He found her sprawled on the bed, her throat slashed to the bone. In her right hand she held a razor, which suggested she had committed suicide. However, a police surgeon was soon able to determine that there was no way that the wound, which was extremely deep, could have been self inflicted. This suggested murder.

Also known as Angelina, for the last three months the victim had been living with dockworker, 24-year-old Frederick Burden. A search was set up for the man, who had fled the area having failed to turn up for work that morning, and while the hunt went on detectives discovered a little more about the suspect and the victim.

From speaking to neighbours they learned that relations between the couple had been fraught with violent quarrels, mainly due to the woman's past. The daughter of a brothel keeper, Lena Faithfull had walked out on her husband in 1893 and gone to live on the streets for over two years, before she persuaded Burden to set up home with her. Burden's friends and family were horrified and tried their best to persuade him against doing so, but he refused to listen. They had then turned against him.

Although he was aware of her past and the fact that she would still occasionally entertain clients when he was at work, it appeared that Burden was very much enamoured with her. Despite this, he had threatened on more than one occasion that if she was to ever leave him, she would do so 'with some limb gone!'

On Wednesday evening, 19 February, they had a fierce row, the culmination of several days of constant quarrelling. Neighbours heard him threaten her – then silence. She was last seen alive at 7 p.m.

SHOCKING TRAGEDY NEAR SOUTHAMPTON.

The murder of Angelina Faithfull recorded in the Illustrated Police News. (*Author's Collection*)

The hunt for the wanted man was to last over a week. When the search failed to locate him it was believed he had either drowned himself in the docks or managed to flee across to the Continent. However, late on the evening of Saturday 29 February Burden was picked up close to his father's home and taken into custody. He said that since leaving Southampton he had slept rough in hayricks and outbuildings on farms in Romsey and Salisbury. Bloodstains were found on his clothing, and he was charged with murder.

When Burden appeared before Mr Justice Day at Winchester Assizes at the end of June, the jury could not agree on a verdict. After deliberating for three hours they were dismissed and a re-trial ordered. This time, before the same judge, the court heard how both the accused and the dead woman were addicted to drink – and how, following a series of quarrels, he had killed her by cutting her throat.

Burden had then placed the razor in her hand to make it appear she had committed suicide. This action, the prosecution suggested, showed that it was wilful murder; by trying to suggest suicide, they pointed out, he was trying to avoid detection. They also claimed that this would destroy any defence of insanity because a man would have to be aware of the seriousness of his actions and the consequences of committing the crime by trying to cover it up.

Burden's defence was that the real killer was one of the numerous male friends who called on Mrs Faithfull while he was at work. After discovering her dead in bed, he told the court, he had fled in a panic as he knew neighbours had heard them quarrelling and felt sure he would be wrongly arrested.

While the jury at his first trial had been unable to reach a verdict, at the second trial they needed less than twenty minutes to reach a verdict, and this time he was convicted and sentenced to death.

14

THROUGH MY OWN TEMPER

Samuel Edward Smith, 21 July 1896

On Wednesday 27 May, 18-year-old Samuel Smith, a private in the 4th Kings Royal Rifles, based at Tournay Barracks, North Camp, Aldershot, was reported and ordered to appear before his commanding officer for 'appearing on parade in a dirty uniform'. The following morning, Smith was absent from early parade and as a result 25-year-old Cpl Robert Payne was ordered to warn Smith he would face further punishment for the offence. When he spoke to Smith the private muttered an insolent reply.

A short time later, Cpl Payne finished his breakfast and was sitting on the edge of a table in the barrack room peeling potatoes for dinner. Payne was chatting to a number of other soldiers in the room when Smith casually sauntered in, holding his rifle as if he was cleaning it. Pte Smith walked behind where Payne was sitting and, without uttering a word, took aim and shot him in the neck, just below the right ear. Payne's lifeless body slumped onto the floor. He had died instantly, without making a sound. Smith was quickly overpowered and taken to the guardroom where he was handed over to the police.

An inquest was held on the following afternoon. PC Knight gave evidence, stating that when Smith asked if he wished to be present at the inquest he replied, 'I don't care whether I am or not,' and then said that he would not attend. In due course Smith appeared before Mr Justice Day at Winchester Assizes at the end of June. His defence was the lack of an obvious motive, and the assertion that the gun had been discharged accidentally. He had initially pleaded guilty to the charge, but on the advice of the judge, his counsel, Mr R. Seton KC, changed his plea to not guilty.

The prosecution claimed it was a cold, premeditated murder carried out by Smith against his superior officer. They claimed that Smith had complained to a comrade that the corporal was 'down upon him.' The court heard that Payne had previously reported Smith for various minor offences, including the one on the day before the murder, but other than that there was no real motive to be found.

Summing up, Mr Justice Day agreed that there was no motive suggested but said that that was no defence against a murder charge, and he also noted that the prisoner had shown no contrition since the shooting and that evidence clearly showed he had vowed to 'get his own back'. The jury took just a few minutes to reach their verdict and Smith was sentenced to death. From the condemned cell Smith penned numerous letters to his mother in which he admitted his guilt and blamed himself for Payne's untimely demise, stating it was 'through my own temper.'

On Tuesday 21 July 1896, the last triple execution in Britain took place. Smith was hanged alongside Philip Matthews (see chapter 12) and Frederick Burden (see chapter 13). Hangman James Billington and assistant William Wilkinson had recently carried out a triple execution at London's Newgate Gaol where there had been an incident on the scaffold which had resulted in Wilkinson falling through the trapdoors when the drop fell; he only saved himself from a nasty injury by grabbing hold of one of the prisoners.

There was no such incident at Winchester. Billington rigged a drop of 7ft 4ins for Matthews, 7ft 6ins for Burden, and 7ft 3ins for Smith. On the morning of the execution all three men awaited their fates bravely. Billington and assistant Wilkinson pinioned each prisoner in turn and all three prisoners walked to the gallows in one long procession. Billington had crudely chalked a large M, B and S from left to right on the trapdoors beneath the corresponding nooses.

Pte Samuel Smith. (Author's Collection)　　*Corporal Robert Payne. (T.J. Leech Archive)*

Cpl Payne's murder made the front page of Illustrated Police News. *(Author's Collection)*

Once the men had crossed the threshold of the scaffold Billington reached out and threw the caps the three had been wearing to one side. Smith was the first to be placed onto the gallows and as Wilkinson placed a strap around his ankles Billington placed a hood over his head then secured the noose. He repeated this with Burden, who took his place in the centre of the traps, and finally Matthews stepped onto the traps and lined his toes to the chalk mark beneath the noose rigged up for him. He bowed farewell to the warders who had sat with him in the condemned cell before the hood was placed over his head and the noose fastened in place. With three men noosed and ready Billington swiftly tugged each rope, checking that the knot was in the correct position, before stepping back and pushing the lever. The three men dropped to their doom and each rope quivered slightly, but there was no sign of any struggle and in the case of each of the men death was instantaneous.

15

RULED BY THE MOON

Charles Maidment, 18 July 1899

It was a tempestuous relationship. Charles Maidment, a 22-year-old market gardener from Swanwick, near Faverham, had been courting Dorcas Houghton for a little over a year but, despite there clearly being much affection between them, they seemed to spend much of their time together quarrelling. As a result the pretty 18-year-old decided enough was enough, and on Tuesday 17 April 1899, Dorcas confided in her mother that she meant to have no more to do with him, and later that day she told Maidment there was no future in their relationship and she was didn't want to see him again.

On the following evening she left her home to visit her sister, who lived nearby at Swanscombe Terrace, Swanwick, and as she strolled along the quiet footpath, her head deep in the book she was reading, she was passed by postman Henry Fielder walking in the opposite direction. Fielder exchanged pleasantries with the young lady before walking on. As Dorcas reached the end of the footpath she found herself face-to-face with Charles Maidment.

The rejected lover, knowing her usual routine, was leaning against a gate and appeared to be waiting for her. She hesitated as she approached but could not simply walk past without speaking. Maidment had brooded for the last twenty-four hours and begged her to reconsider and take him back. His words fell on deaf ears and finally, when he could see he was getting nowhere, he pulled out a gun and fired once, the bullet striking her in the head, fatally wounding her.

Hearing a shot, Henry Fielder turned and rushed back down the path – where he was horrified to find Miss Houghton lying in a pool of blood by the roadside. Immediately he raised an alarm and while police hurried to the scene a message was sent to Dr Cade of Salisbury, who certified she was dead and that the cause of death was a bullet that had entered her head behind the left ear.

After firing the shot Maidment had climbed over a fence and fled, heading towards Fareham. A short time later he approached a police constable and asked, 'Is this the police station?' Told it was, he made for the door and entered. The constable followed him inside and asked what he wanted. Maidment made no reply, but reached into his pocket, and placing the six-barrelled revolver onto the counter, declared, 'You had better keep me here.'

The following morning Maidment was brought up at Fareham Police Court charged with the wilful murder of Dorcas Houghton. He appeared deeply dejected and made no comment to the charge, which was read out in the empty courtroom; local newspapers recorded that there was 'not a single spectator in the dingy court.'

When Maidment stood trial before Mr Justice Wright at Hampshire Assizes at the end of June the prosecution's case was that it was a deliberate, premeditated, cold-blooded murder by a spurned lover. Maidment's affection for the girl was not reciprocated and when she broke off the relationship he shot her in a jealous frenzy. On the point of premeditation, the prosecution counsel showed that shortly before the murder Maidment had spoken to a young boy in the village who had asked if he knew of any work. Maidment apparently told him, 'I dare say if you go down to Tucker's (Maidment's place of work) in about a week's time you'll be able to get a job.'

Dorcas Houghton.
(Author's
Collection)

DECLARATION OF SHERIFF
AND OTHERS.

31 *Vict. Cap.* 24.

We, the undersigned, hereby declare that Judgment of Death was this Day executed on *Chas Maidment* in Her Majesty's Prison of *Winchester* in our presence.

Dated this *18th* day of *July 1899*

Thos H. Woodham acting Under Sheriff of *Hants*

_____Justice of the Peace

for_____

J. Dodgs Gov. Governor of the said Prison.

J. A. Ladbrooke Chaplain of the said Prison.

PRINTED AT H. M. CONVICT PRISON, CHATHAM.

Above left: *Charles Maidment. (Author's Collection)*

Above right: *Notice that Charles Maidment had been executed. (Author's Collection)*

His defence was insanity. His counsel claimed that Maidment was 'ruled by the moon' and his behaviour was noticeably different when there was a full moon, during which time he became morose and sullen. The court heard of that he had obtained the gun in the previous year, to use for sport, and while learning to fire it he shot himself in the hand. The jury were told that there was a long history of insanity in Maidment's family and that a number of cousins had been, or currently were, residing in a local asylum.

Despite a spirited defence, the jury needed just ten minutes to agree with the prosecution's version of events, that Maidment was a cold-blooded murderer, and found him guilty as charged. Once sentence of death had been passed on him he was taken to the condemned cell at Winchester where, a few days before he was to go to the gallows, he was visited by two medical experts from the Home Office. It seemed the defence's view that the prisoner was insane was being investigated further but, following a number of tests, they were convinced that there was nothing in the prisoner's mental condition to save him from the gallows.

16

'MAD IN DRINK'

William Churcher, 22 July 1902

Sir,

I hope, please God, that you will take my case into your kind and merciful consideration
and look it over for my sake as I could never have known what I was doing at the time for
I was mad in drink at the time or it would never have happened …

Petition for mercy by Bill Churcher following his conviction for murder.

In July 1898, 26-year-old Sophia Jane Hepworth married her husband William, a
tailor, and they were living in South Street, Gosport. Less than four months into the
marriage she rekindled a relationship with William 'Bill' Churcher, a labourer some
five years older with whom she had lived, on and off, for the previous decade. Leaving
her husband, the couple took lodgings elsewhere in the town, but Hepworth soon
tracked them down and persuaded his wife to return to him.

No sooner had she left than Churcher was hot on her heels and, arriving at South
Street, he made a number of threats, which resulted in Sophia Hepworth leaving her
husband and accompanying Churcher back to his lodgings. This scenario was played
out a further five times over the following years: she would pack her bags and return
to her husband only for Churcher to follow her and persuade her to go back to him at
his home at 16 Clarence Buildings, one of a block of small dwellings in a courtyard off
North Street, close to the harbour at Alverstoke and occupied by what the newspapers
reported as 'the lower class'.

Both Churcher and Mrs Hepworth were fond of a drink, but it was she who was
prone to drunken outbursts and aggression when drunk. At Easter-time of 1902 Sophia
Hepworth became convinced that Churcher was having a relationship with the
daughter of a neighbour at Clarence Buildings, and on the night of Wednesday 9 April
1902 the situation reached crisis point.

The couple spent the evening in a public house at Alverstoke and, as they began to
get more drunk, the topic again turned to his alleged infidelity. Churcher continued to

deny any such impropriety, but it appears she chose not to believe him. At closing time they began to make their way home and, as they entered the courtyard at Clarence Buildings, she suddenly darted across the yard and headed for the exit, which led to the harbour. A crowd watched as she approached the sea and then waded into the water.

Churcher gave chase and seeing her enter the water he followed and dragged her out, tearing her skirt in the process.

He then took her back to their lodgings, with her kicking and struggling all the while. Though he closed the front door behind them, neighbours could hear an argument, punctuated by shouts, the smashing of glass and the sound of furniture being slammed about. The disturbance finally reached a climax at around 1.45 a.m., when, after a piercing scream, the house fell into silence.

Churcher was seen to leave Clarence Buildings later that morning, locking the door and walking quickly away. There was nothing more heard from the residents of No. 16 all day Thursday; the blinds stayed drawn and there were no comings or goings at the house. When this silence continued into the following day, Good Friday, neighbours became concerned and, when Sophia failed to keep an appointment, the police were contacted.

Officers were already in possession of the torn part of Sophia's skirt from when she was rescued from the sea, and in the pocket was a foreign coin and a key. Police Sergeant Hawkins was detailed to investigate and arrived at Clarence Buildings at 2.30 p.m. Entering the house using the recovered key, he found Sophia Hepworth lying dead in a pool of blood, flecked with pieces of smashed china, on the floor: her throat had been cut and there were numerous cuts and stab wounds to her arms and upper body. Her head had been rested on a cushion from the adjacent chair and she was fully clothed except for the remaining part of her torn skirt, which had been used to cover the body.

Churcher was arrested in a Gosport public house later that evening, and immediately made a full confession. 'Yes, it's a funny job,' he told PC Loder, who arrested him. He then pulled out a clasp knife which he gave to the officer, telling him that this was the murder weapon, and he also gave the officer eight dog licences asking him to give them to his brother and to ask him to take his dog and all his possessions from the murder house.

Churcher was detained at Portsmouth Gaol pending trial and while being transported by ferry to a remand hearing at Gosport a week later he attempted to take his own life by jumping overboard: with his hands cuffed he was unable to swim and sank into the water. A boat was quickly launched and Churcher was pulled to safety and taken to court.

Appearing before Mr Justice Bigham at Hampshire Assizes, Winchester, on 28 June, Churcher pleaded not guilty, although he had never denied the crime since his arrest and had claimed he had been greatly provoked. Several witnesses testified and although there was much evidence to support provocation, it was also heard that Churcher had assaulted Sophia on numerous occasions, that she frequently sported black eyes, and that on the night of her death, neighbours heard her pleading, 'Don't murder me, Bill!'

Churcher said he had only resorted to stabbing after she had thrown a number of vases at him and had attempted to stab him with the knife. The numerous cuts to her arms and upper body suggested that she had struggled to fight off the attacker; the fatal wound, a

GOSPORT TRAGEDY.

Accused Found Guilty and Sentenced to Death.

RECOMMENDED TO MERCY.

To-day, at the Winchester Assizes, the man William Churcher, aged 35, described as a labourer, was indicted for murdering Sophia Jane Hepworth, at Alverstoke, on April 10th.

Mr. Evan Austen and Mr. E. B. Charles (instructed by Messrs. G. H. King and Franckeiss, on behalf of the Treasury) conducted the case for the prosecution, and, at the request of the Judge, the prisoner was defended by Mr. W. J. H. Brodrick.

STORY OF THE CRIME.

The evidence given at the inquest and before the Gosport magistrates revealed a shocking story. In July, 1898, the murdered woman was married to William Hepworth, a tailor, living at 5, Trinity-view, South-street, Gosport. At that time the woman was 26 years old. Four

A newspaper report of the Gosport Murder. (Author's Collection)

4ins cut to the throat which had severed her windpipe and jugular vein, was so deep that it had almost decapitated her. It had been carried out with such violence that it clearly suggested murder. The jury agreed and needed an absence of just thirty minutes to find the prisoner guilty as charged. However, they did add a recommendation for mercy.

Churcher penned a passionate plea for his life to the Home Secretary in which he claimed he was 'mad in drink'. While it may have been the case that the victim was very drunk on the night of the murder, it was alleged that Churcher had not been. It was noted on his plea that he was not 'mad in drink' and although Churcher ended his letter by saying that the jury had 'strongly, strongly, strongly' recommended him to mercy it was seemingly felt he was using being drunk as an excuse for the murder and his letter was ignored.

He was hanged by William Billington. It was one of the last executions carried out without the aid of an assistant and the first in Great Britain that was heralded by the tolling of a prison bell instead of the hoisting of a black flag.

17

PARTNERS IN CRIME

William Brown & Thomas Cowdrey, 16 December 1903

As the days to the execution were counted down, there was a great deal of disquiet at the impending sentence being carried out. The two men who were to hang side by side had been convicted of a brutal murder and robbery during a sexual assault and, while it was felt that in the case of one of the men there should be nothing to prevent the law taking its course, in the case of the other it seemed that a miscarriage of justice was about to take place.

On the morning of the execution, as the two were led to the scaffold, coming face-to-face for the last time, one spoke as hangman William Billington moved to place the noose around his neck.

'Before I leave this world, I wish to say that I helped to do it,' said Brown. His partner in crime, standing close by on the trapdoors, then interrupted, 'Give me five minutes to tell the truth!' He then paused as if to gather his thoughts and continued, 'God help my innocence. I'm going to Heaven. Brown did it, he has said so …' At that, the hangman and his assistant moved swiftly and moments later the curtain came down on a brutal crime that caused controversy not just in Hampshire but over 600 miles away in the north of Scotland.

Thirty-five-year-old Esther Atkins earned her living as a prostitute, frequenting the various pubs and cafés popular with soldiers from the numerous barracks and army camps in Aldershot. Late on the night of Tuesday 6 October 1903, she was in the Crimea Inn when she picked up three men; two serving and one former soldier. The soldiers were in the grey overcoats and Glengarry patterned caps of the 2nd Royal Scots Fusiliers, based at the Mandora Barracks.

Shortly before midnight, cab driver Robert Carter picked up the four passengers: the two soldiers got inside with the woman whilst the other man climbed up onto the driver's seat next to the driver and soon made his intentions clear, boasting that the woman had about £10 and he meant to take it from her.

Carter, known in the town as 'Blind Bob' and whose licence had recently been revoked, was shocked at such a blatant admission and, turning to look at the passenger, he mentally noted his appearance before they reached their destination. They asked the cabman to drop them off at the Red Church on Beuley Road and they headed towards a place known locally as The Coppice.

At two o'clock on the following morning, 36-year-old labourer and former fusilier Thomas Cowdrey approached a man named William Smith outside the Engineer's stables, a mile or so from The Coppice, and told him he had just had a narrow escape. Cowdrey said that he had been walking beside a churchyard when he heard a woman screaming and when he went to investigate he saw two soldiers attacking a woman. Going to investigate, Cowdrey said he was struck about the head and arms as he fought off the attack, being told to keep away as this was none of his business. He told Smith that as there was nothing he could do to help he decided to flee, but not before picking up the woman's stays, which were lying on the ground close to where the struggle was taking place.

Smith advised him to inform the military police and a short time later he spoke to Provost Marshal Maj. Wood, who in turn notified the civilian police. Before dawn Cowdrey had repeated his story to a sergeant in the Aldershot police before accompanying him to where he said he had seen the woman being attacked. Here the police, in the company of a local doctor, found the battered body of Esther Atkins: almost naked and a mass of bruises, including several to her wrists. It seemed she had fought in vain for her life and that her assailants had held her down by her wrists. Cowdrey stood back, refusing to approach the body. The doctor concurred that she had been attacked by at least one man.

At first light the Aldershot police decided to see if Cowdrey, formerly an inmate in an asylum and already known to local officers as someone of low intelligence, could spot the soldiers at the nearby barracks. He said that he was unable to identify the uniforms of his attackers, nor did he recognise their regiment. The woman had been battered to death with the branch of a tree and the heavy brass buckles of a belt and also sexually assaulted. Missing from her were her stays and shoes.

William Brown and John Dunbar photographed at the remand court. (T.J. Leech Archive)

Maj. Woods, of the military police, had also been doing some investigating and soon had two suspects in custody. Woods interviewed a number of soldiers asking if anyone had noticed anything suspicious and one, Pte John Robinson, stated that two Scottish soldiers, 27-year-old William Brown of Ayrshire, and 21-year-old John Dunbar of Montrose, had returned to barracks at 12.15 a.m. on the Wednesday morning and Brown had asked for a towel so he could wipe his hands. Robinson noticed that his hands were bloodstained. Brown and Dunbar should have been confined to barracks on the night of the murder but it was soon clear that they had been in the town, and, when questioned and searched, Brown was found to be in possession of a pair of women's shoes.

On Thursday morning a second identity parade was set up, and this time Cowdrey picked out William Brown as one of his attackers. Brown was arrested and charged. Cowdrey had failed to identify Dunbar. When questioned by Maj. Woods, Dunbar confessed that he and Brown had broken out of barracks, just after 9.30 p.m. on the Tuesday, and that they had been to the Crimea Inn, where they met with Esther Atkins – and also, they claimed, with the informant Cowdrey. Dunbar was arrested and charged with murder and a week later, following further investigations, William Cowdrey was recognised by cab driver Carter as being the third man he had picked up in the company of the murdered woman. Carter had already identified Brown and Dunbar as two of the men he had driven to the Red Church. Cowdrey pleaded his innocence, but an examination of his clothing found strong traces of blood. He claimed that it must have got onto his clothing when he had directed police to the murder scene, but it was already noted that Cowdrey had made a point of staying away from where the woman had been found at The Coppice.

At the end of November all three stood in the dock before Mr Justice Wills at Winchester Assizes accused of wilful murder. The trial was to last for four days, with each man blaming the others for what had happened. It was shown that Brown, along with a woman friend, had been in the company of the Esther Atkins on the morning of the murder, and that after receiving a payment from a client she had put it inside her stays, telling them that this was were she kept her money.

Brown admitted that he and Dunbar had gone to The Coppice with the woman for the usual purposes and after they had sex he saw Cowdrey approach and claim that the woman was carrying a large sum of money. Brown then admitted that he had helped Cowdrey to attack the woman.

As a result both Brown and Cowdrey were found guilty and sentenced to death. John Dunbar, who admitted being present but claimed that he had been unaware that there had been any plan to rob or attack the woman, and who was found to have taken no part in the attack, was acquitted of all charges and walked from the court a free man.

Following his release Dunbar began a campaign to save the life of his fellow countryman, claiming that it was Cowdrey alone who had committed the murder and robbery, and, although papers north of the border took up the case and tried to get the conviction quashed, the Home Secretary had already learned of Brown's confession and refused to interfere with the due process of law.

Left: *William Billington.*
(Author's Collection)

Below: *How the* Illustrated
Police News *recorded the*
execution of Brown and
Cowdrey. (T.J. Leech Archive)

WILLIAM BROWN.

THOMAS COWDREY.

18

A FAMILY AFFAIR

Augustus John Penny, 26 November 1913

In the years leading up to the First World War, the picturesque village of Copythorne, at the head of the New Forest, a few miles to the west of Totton, boasted just a few hundred inhabitants. Residing in a picturesque, ivy-clad, cottage at Pollard's Moor, with large gardens was the Penny family, comprising of brothers George, aged 34, Augustus, aged 30, and their 57-year-old mother, Mary. Despite this idyllic and peaceful setting there was animosity and bad blood amongst the family. For one thing, their mother was a cantankerous drunk who frequently quarrelled with anyone who happened to cross her, but the main butt of her aggression seemed to be her younger son Augustus, who preferred to be known as Gus, and on more than one occasion she had been summonsed for assaulting him.

In his mid-teens, Gus Penny, tired of the domestic disharmony that had already caused their father to leave home and move to Portsmouth, decided to enlist in the navy. He served twelve years in the senior service before returning to Copythorne and finding work as a farm labourer.

Besides the family home, Mrs Penny also owned 7½ acres of local farmland and, as a result of this impending inheritance, Gus Penny seemed prepared to put up with the domestic situation. However, in January 1913, Mrs Penny sowed further disharmony when she rented the farmland to George in return for a nominal weekly income. Gus Penny was enraged and from then on their arguments became far worse. Matters came to a head in June when Gus Penny announced he was giving up work and would spend his time idling and drinking.

In the early hours of Sunday morning, 22 June, Penny acquired a hunting-rifle from a neighbour, saying he wanted to shoot pigeons. He returned to the cottage and breakfasted, even taking a cup of tea up to his mother, who was in bed, and for the rest of that day relations seemed good between all members of the family.

That evening George Penny went to the pub where he worked as a part-time barman, finishing his shift shortly before 11 p.m. Arriving back home George looked in on his mother, who was in bed, and appeared to be fast asleep. He then stopped by his brother's room – where he could hear the sounds of sobbing. Looking through the open door he saw Gus lying on his bed, head buried in his hands, repeatedly crying 'Oh dear... oh dear!'. Believing his brother drunk, George left him in peace and went to bed.

When he woke on the following morning he found his brother had gone. When there was no movement from his mother's room George went to investigate and was greeted with a horrific sight. Daylight revealed that Mrs Penny was lying dead on her bed with the bedroom walls splattered with blood.

George hurried to fetch the local policeman, PC Sidney Joyce, stationed in the neighbouring village of Cadnam, and an extensive search of the surrounding area was quickly organised. They were helped by local residents and one of them, 11-year-old Evelyn Light, said he had seen the wanted man climb out of a well and run towards a hedge in a nearby field. Gus Penny was soon located crouching beneath the hedge on Pollard's Moor, less than a quarter of a mile from the cottage.

Taken to Lyndhurst police station, Penny initially told the police that the gun had gone off by accident, but a few days later he asked to see Superintendent Harry Wakeford, who led the murder inquiry. Looking depressed and downcast Penny then made the following statement:

> Last Sunday I got up about 4 o'clock – took the gun I had borrowed on the Saturday night and went into our meadow to try and shoot pigeons, but I could not get any. I shot and wounded one but could not find it. I returned home about 7 o'clock and got the breakfast. My brother George returned about eight o'clock. I poured out the tea and took some up to my mother, then me and George sat down and had breakfast together. George and myself got the cabbage and potatoes ready, I put it in the pot. George left home about eleven, I then again went into the fields to look for the wounded pigeon, but could not find it. I again returned home.

Penny then went on to say that one of the locals came over for a haircut. His brother was also the local barber, but since George wasn't at home, Gus did the job. Penny and his mother had lunch and at 2 p.m. Gus went out for a drink and returned soon afterwards. He said he and his mother had their tea at five. George came in an hour later and had his tea. Mrs Penny asked for the money for her beer. After George had

Far left:
Penny's house at Pollard's Moor, Copythorne.
(T.J. Leech Archive)

Left: *Gus Penny (centre) being taken into custody. (T.J. Leech Archive)*

gone out, Gus himself then also went out for a drink, but came back at about half-past eight with some beer for Mrs Penny. She was in bed and he took the drink up for her. The good spirit of that Sunday seemed to be holding and the pair shared a drink and he put an old coat on her feet, as she said they were cold.

Penny then told the police that his mother's mood had suddenly changed and she began abusing him. She said if it were not for George she wouldn't have money for drink, that she would like to see Gus becoming a tramp, and that she was going to sell their hay, so that she and George could leave Copythorne and leave Gus behind. She told him he could 'go to the Devil'.

Penny said that he had tried to tell his mother to be quiet and go to sleep, but he said that she kept taunting him about his brother and kept on and on and on. 'I lost all control of myself,' Penny continued, 'I went to my bedroom, got the gun and before I could cool my temper I shot her in the head.' Penny ended by telling officers that he hadn't intended to kill his mother, and that he was now very sorry, dramatically adding, 'I must suffer for it.'

Augustus Penny was charged with murder and appeared before Commissioner Frederick Low KC at the Winchester Assizes on Saturday 8 November. The public gallery was crowded, while Penny, as a mark of respect to his dead mother, sported a black tie and armband. He pleaded 'not guilty' to murder, claiming that he had been provoked. Opening the case for the Crown, Mr G.W. Ricketts KC told the court that this was a cold-blooded murder caused by the resentment the prisoner felt for his brother being effectively given the land.

George Penny told the court that his mother had split from her husband who now lived in Portsmouth and while on naval service his brother would often stay with his father. He said that after the agreement about the land, gradually Augustus had become more and more bitter. He explained that when he returned from the pub himself after work, the house was in darkness. He also said that he had no idea when his brother had brought a gun into the cottage. With regards to Gus's attitude, George told the court that he often made threats and he and his mother ignored him. He also thought he should say that when his brother was 'in drink' he was often quite mad.

Police Sergeant Ernest Long gave evidence that he tested the murder rifle and it had a double pull, which meant it required much more effort to fire it, and he concluded it could not be fired by accident.

Penny was defended by Mr Blake Odgers KC, who told the court that the accused had served his country well in the navy for some twelve years from the age of 16. He said that in 1911 Penny returned home and lived on and off with his mother. Odgers called Superintendent Wakeford and questioned him about Mrs Penny. The officer stated that she had a number of convictions against her, including one in 1906 for physically abusing her children. Odgers told the court that it was due to her drinking that her husband had left her. Indeed the superintendent said that he agreed with the defence counsel, who considered the prisoner 'a good son to a bad mother'. The court also heard that at one time Mrs Penny had gone into the workhouse, and it was her son Gus that had taken her out.

In response to this Mr Ricketts said the jury should hear that George had said that his brother had also assaulted their mother. The judge interjected and said it was only

Hangman John Ellis. (Author's Collection)

fair that the jury should know that the convictions by Mrs Penny for hitting her son were when he was just 13 and 14. Odgers then said that he would not be calling any direct evidence for the defence.

In his summing-up Mr Ricketts said the jury should remember that Penny left the room, returned with a gun, and shot his mother – not in the heat of any direct argument. Whatever sympathy the jury might feel for the accused, this was not legal provocation.

Mr Odgers then made his final address to the court saying that he would make an unashamed plea for his client's life. He said the jury could now see that Penny was basically 'a good man', who could not have premeditatedly murdered his mother. He said there was no evidence that he had obtained the gun with murder in his mind. Odgers suggested Penny had become carried away in a moment of passion when under the influence of drink. Were not his cries of 'oh dear' those of severe remorse, he asked the jury?

In his final address, Commissioner Row said if the jury believed the prisoner had fired the gun, and bearing in mind Mrs Penny was a defenceless woman, then they should not 'shrink from doing their duty to the public, even though a man's life lay in their hands.' At the end of the day-long trial the jury were out for just twenty-five minutes, before returning to court. However, they did not deliver a verdict immediately. The foreman asked the judge for clarity regarding the difference between murder and manslaughter. The judge also re-affirmed that there was no evidence that this was an accident.

The jury then returned and the foreman said they had agreed upon their verdict: they found the prisoner guilty of murder, but as the black cap was being draped onto the judge's wig he added, 'My Lord, we recommend him to mercy.' Once the prisoner had been removed from the dock the judge asked the jury why they had recommended mercy, and was told, 'On the character of the mother and the probable provocation he received.'

Penny's legal team declined to appeal, deciding instead to petition the Home Secretary, Reginald McKenna, for mercy. None was shown, and Penny kept an early morning appointment with hangman John Ellis.

19

BECAUSE OF HER PAST

Walter James White, 16 June 1914

W alter White was perplexed when he found his girlfriend being treated in such an off-hand manner and refused entry by the landlady at her brother's lodging house at Gilfarch, Glamorgan. The 22-year-old decorator from Swindon had been courting 24-year-old Frances Priscilla Hunter for several months and, believing she was the one for him, he had broached the subject of marriage with her and her responses had been favourable. The visit to meet members of her family in Wales further strengthened their relationship, but the trip was to set a chain of events into action that would cost the lives of the two lovers.

Unbeknown to White, Frances Hunter had something of a past. After a messy love affair, in which she had run off with a former employer, a married man, and lived with him for a while as man and wife, Frances, a native of Devizes, had then moved to Swindon where she had met and fallen in love with White. Following his tentative promises of marriage she resolved to tell him of her past, but whenever she tried to broach the subject she stalled.

The visit to Glamorgan took place at the end of April 1914, and when she called on her brother the landlady refused them entry, telling White that she would not have a woman like Frances Hunter under her roof. The landlady, a Mrs Blewitt, stubbornly refused to allow Frances entry to her house, nor would she explain to White why, but when he later asked her in private, she said if he gave her his address she would write and explain.

A few days later a letter arrived in Swindon from Mrs Blewitt and, while the contents did not explain why she had refused his sweetheart entry to her house, it did contain the offer that if White cared to visit her again, alone, she would be more forthcoming. White caught a train to Wales. What he was to hear broke his heart.

Mrs Blewitt told him about Frances's past, and made clear her disapproval at what she believed immoral and unacceptable behaviour. White also looked disapprovingly upon such conduct, and believed that the woman he took for his wife should be chaste and pure. Equally upsetting was the fact that Frances had failed to reveal anything about her past to him when they had discussed marriage. In his eyes she had deceived him, and what he had learned from Mrs Blewitt had destroyed him.

Walter White. (T.J. Leech Archive)

Frances Hunter, who was shot dead by Walter White. (T.J. Leech Archive)

The Goddard Arms Hotel Swindon, where White committed murder. (T.J. Leech Archive)

White returned to Swindon, where he wrote letters to his mother, and to Frances' father, in which he claimed that his sweetheart had ruined his life and that he was going to meet his Maker. The letter to her father was even more to the point. He claimed that his refusal to speak had 'killed two lives.'

He then acquired a gun and set out for the Goddard Arms Hotel, in Swindon's Old Town, where Frances was employed as a maid. At 6 p.m. on Wednesday 29 April, he arrived at the hotel and asked to speak to Frances alone. A number of her colleagues saw them leave the hotel by a back door and enter an outbuilding in a yard at the rear of the inn. Moments later three shots rang out. The manager rushed across the yard where he found Frances lying dead in the coalhouse with White standing over her, revolver in hand. White turned to the manager, calmly asking him to contact the police.

White offered no resistance when detectives arrived at the hotel and he later made a statement in which he claimed he had done what he had done after receiving the letter from Mrs Blewitt. He said that when he called at the hotel he confronted Frances with what the landlady had told him and asked if it was true. Tears streamed down her face as she admitted it was, and at that White pulled out the gun and told her he was going to kill her so that she would never deceive anyone ever again. He said that she had simply looked at him and said, 'For God's sake do it then!' White said that she had then kissed him goodbye; he aimed the gun and shot her.

His trial took place before Mr Justice Ridley at Wells Assizes on 28 May. Prosecution counsel Rayner Goddard KC told the court that it was a case of a cruel, premeditated murder of a lover who had been upset at something he had learned about the woman he had hoped to marry. In anger and jealousy he had shot her dead.

His defence was that the brutal nature of the crime showed clearly that White was in such a perturbed state of mind that he was not responsible for his actions. The jury believed that it was a case of wilful murder although, in reaching their decision, they did offer a strong recommendation for mercy.

The judge noted on the file that he did not support the recommendation and White's appeal, heard a few weeks later, was soon dismissed. The Home Secretary considered the case and noted that although White had previously been of good character, the fact that he had written the letters in which he mentioned that he intended to commit the crime, and had acquired a gun and called to see Frances at the place where he shot her dead, showed premeditation. There was therefore no reason why the law should not take its course.

20

FOR THE SAKE OF PLUNDER

Leo George O'Donnell, 29 March 1917

Lieutenant William Frederick Watterton had completed his military service and had retired on a pension, only to rejoin the army when war broke out. He took up the position of quartermaster at the Isolation Hospital, Aldershot, living in the steward's quarters with his daughter. On the evening of New Year's Day 1917, 22-year-old Leo O'Donnell, an Irish born sergeant in the Royal Army Medical Corps, called to see 48-year-old Watterton, seeking permission to marry the lieutenant's daughter, whom he had been courting for several months.

Once permission was granted he quickly informed his sweetheart, who immediately made plans to celebrate the news. Miss Watterton, serving in the Women's Auxiliary Service, obtained a night pass so that she could celebrate her engagement with a girlfriend. She went out at shortly after 8 p.m., leaving her father and fiancé talking and after several drinks, the girls returned at 9.30 p.m. and found Watterton was not at home. This was something of a surprise as he had told his daughter he was tired and planned to have an early night. The girls decided to wait up for him and at 11.30 p.m. O'Donnell called and told them that the lieutenant had left earlier that night for an urgent appointment. There were a number of things that caused the girl to be suspicious of her new fiancé.

Firstly, he had been wearing boots when she had last seen him at 8 p.m. and now he was wearing shoes, and he also mentioned that he had left a wooden truncheon when he had visited earlier and that it seemed to have vanished. He also had brown stains on his hands. When she questioned what they were he said he had been 'developing' and she assumed he meant photographs.

When her father failed to return home by midnight they contacted the military police and at lunchtime on the following day the body of William Watterton was found in a trench on a nearby training ground. He had been battered to death and his pockets had been rifled. A post-mortem later found he had sustained over twenty wounds to his head and that death had taken place sometime on the previous evening. This timing was supported by the fact that during Watterton's frantic struggle for his life, his watch had been smashed. It had stopped at exactly nine o'clock. The post-mortem found that

Above left: *Lt William Watterton.* (*Author's Collection*)

Above right: *The* Illustrated Police News' *account of the discovery of Lt Watterton's body.* (*T.J. Leech Archive*)

the injuries were consistent with having been inflicted by a blunt instrument such as a truncheon or a heavy stone, similar to the bloodstained rock that had been recovered from beside the body.

The military passed the investigation into the hands of the Hampshire Constabulary and their prime suspect was Leo O'Donnell. Asked to account for his movements on the night of the murder, O'Donnell claimed that he had gone to the sergeant's mess at about 8.15 p.m., then he had gone on to the Headquarters office building to do some work before going to a social held in the training school. He gave detectives the names of several colleagues who he claimed he had spoken to that night, but when questioned none could substantiate O'Donnell's alibi.

A sergeant at the camp, James Wood, told detectives he was in the sergeant's mess between seven and nine o'clock. As there were so few other people there, he said, he would surely have noticed if O'Donnell had come into the mess at any time that evening. Another soldier then told officers he had seen O'Donnell returning to his barracks some time between ten and eleven o'clock. With inconsistencies in his statement, O'Donnell was arrested and charged.

While on remand at Winchester Gaol O'Donnell tried to get a fellow prisoner to find someone to testify he had been with O'Donnell in Winchester on the night of the murder and that if someone would come forward O'Donnell would pay him £500. He even wrote to Miss Watterton, the murdered man's daughter, asking her to say that they were together at the time of the killing!

Both of these attempts at establishing a false alibi were brought up when O'Donnell stood trial before Mr Justice Darling on 9 February at Winchester Assizes. O'Donnell's defence was handled by Mr H. du Parcq KC, who claimed that the prisoner had not committed the crime and the real killer's motive for the murder was blackmail, involving an illegitimate son.

O'Donnell claimed that shortly before Christmas, Watterton had confided to him that a man had turned up at the camp claiming to be Watterton's son. Watterton had admitted to O'Donnell that he had had an affair with a Spanish girl while serving in Gibraltar and now the young man was blackmailing him. O'Donnell's defence was that the illegitimate son was the murderer.

When questioned about the attempts at establishing a false alibi O'Donnell claimed he was trying to spare his fiancée from hearing the truth about her father's past and told the court that if someone had come forward on his behalf, he would not have mentioned the blackmailing.

The prosecution, led by Mr Clavell Salter KC, said that there was evidence to show that O'Donnell was the man who murdered Lieutenant Watterton. The weapon used to commit the murder was a wooden truncheon, fashioned from an old toilet brush with the bristles removed and which was proved to belong to the accused. He had carried out the brutal attack in order to obtain the keys to the safe in the quartermaster's office so he would be able to steal the contents.

Having committed the murder, and obtained the keys, it was revealed that O'Donnell had called at the hospital and asked to be shown into the quartermaster's office, claiming that Lieutenant Watterton had sent him on an errand. However, although he had taken the safe keys he had not taken the key to the office, and being unable to gain entry he returned to his billet.

The jury were told to treat the stories about the alleged blackmail and the illegitimate son with the contempt they deserved and, after the judge's summing up, they needed just seven minutes to return their verdict of guilty. Passing sentence of death, on the second day of the trial, Mr Justice Darling told O'Donnell that he had been convicted of a cruel and heartless murder committed for the sake of plunder and for no other reason. He then told the prisoner, 'I should be wanting in my duty if I held out to you any sort of hope in this world. You had better make your peace with God!'

Awaiting execution, O'Donnell attacked a warder with a water jug for no reason. The warder was able to fend off the blow and restrain the prisoner and for the following days he remained with his arms tied by his side. He enjoyed a hearty meal on the night before his execution but told the warders he did not want to be served any breakfast on the following morning.

Instead of being issued with his own clothes on the morning of his execution he remained in his prison garb, as the only suit of clothes O'Donnell possessed was his army uniform and it had been decided that no man would be hanged in uniform. Although he had maintained a confident and cocksure attitude throughout his time in the condemned cell, when hangman Ellis entered to pinion his arms he recorded later that he found the prisoner looked painfully white and upset. Because the prison

DECLARATION OF SHERIFF
AND OTHERS.

31 *Vict.* Cap. 24.

We, the undersigned, hereby declare that Judgment of Death was this Day executed on *Leo George O'Donnell* in His Majesty's Prison of *Winchester* in our presence.

Dated this *29th* day of *March 1917*

Ths. H. Woolham Sheriff of *Hampshire*.

Justice of the Peace for _____.

Governor of the said Prison.

C. Chaplain of the said Prison.

No. 280

Above left: *Leo O'Donnell. (Author's Collection)*

Above right: *A notice to show O'Donnell had been executed. (Author's Collection)*

tunic had a high neck Ellis had to pull it back over his shoulders in order to bare his neck. Ellis then left the prisoner in the company of his assistant and assorted warders and hurried to the gallows to await the arrival of the procession. Although it was only a distance of less than 50 yards the last walk took a painfully long time, caused mainly by the pace of the elderly Catholic priest, who was a frail 75 years of age and unable to walk much beyond a slow shuffle. O'Donnell had no choice but to match his pace and as Ellis watched the procession slowly approach he could see that the prisoner had a look of horror on his face at seeing the scaffold and noose awaiting him.

Once they had him on the trapdoors assistant executioner Baxter secured his ankles and stepped back as Ellis swiftly placed the noose and pushed the lever. Seconds before the drop fell O'Donnell swooned in a faint and as a result his body plunged into the pit, striking the sides and leaving the rope swinging violently. It was reported that death was due to asphyxia and not a broken neck.

21

ADDRESS UNKNOWN

Thomas Henry Allaway, 19 August 1922

Lady cook (31) requires post in school. Experience in school with forty boarders. Disengaged. Salary £65. Miss I. Wilkins, 21 Thirlmere Road, Streatham SW 16.

As requested, the advertisement appeared in the *Morning Post*. Irene May Wilkins, the 31-year-old unmarried daughter of a deceased London barrister, was desperately seeking a new job and sent a letter, along with a postal order for 3s, to the advertising manager of the Fleet-Street based newspaper asking for the notice to be placed in the Thursday morning edition, 22 December 1921.

It seemed her appeal had met with immediate success as shortly before lunchtime, a telegram arrived at the house in Streatham. It read, 'Morning Post come immediately 4.30 train Waterloo. Bournemouth Central. Car will meet train expense no object. Urgent. Wood. Beech House.'

Irene immediately replied by telegram to Mr Wood at Beech House accepting the offer and at 3 p.m. she boarded a bus to Waterloo. The southbound express had barely pulled out of the station when the telegram was returned to Irene's home, marked 'address unknown'. In Bournemouth the telegram boy, finding no Beech House listed, had consulted with others in the office and, believing the sender may have made a mistake, was instead told to deliver it to 'Beechhurst' on Beechwood Avenue in the town. At that address lived a Mr Sutton, an invalid in the care of a nurse. The nurse answered the door after the post boy had dropped the telegram onto the doormat and cycled away. The nurse quickly returned it to the sorting office, explaining that there was nobody by the name of Wood living at the house, and it was immediately returned to sender.

Darkness had fallen when Irene Wilkins, carrying her small attaché case, arrived at Bournemouth Central railway station at 7.03 p.m. The train was almost twenty minutes late, but as she exited the station she found a car along with a smartly dressed driver waiting to collect her. She handed the chauffeur her case, which he quickly stowed in the boot, and moments later the car pulled away from the station concourse and headed, Irene assumed, towards her new post at Beech House.

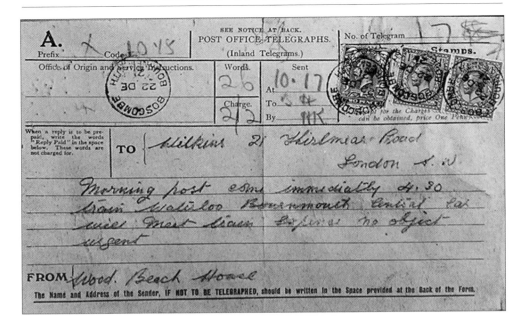

Above: *The telegram sent in reply to Irene Wilkins's newspaper notice. (Author's Collection)*

Left: *Irene Wilkins. (Author's Collection)*

Irene Wilkins's body photographed in the field. (TNA PRO)

Soon after dawn on the following morning, Charles Nicklen, an elderly labourer out walking at a place known locally as Fifteen Acre Meadow, on the outskirts of Boscombe, became aware of two cows nosing at a bundle lying in a field, behind a gorse bush. This unusual sight caused him to take a closer look and he discovered the dead body of a woman; her clothes were disarrayed and her face was a mass of blood and bruises.

Police officers were soon at the scene under the command of Superintendent Shadrach Garrett and, as detectives began their investigations, they already had a possible name for the victim. Irene's family had debated the returned telegram on the previous evening and decided that first thing on the following morning they would report their concerns to the police. Within the hour the name of Irene Wilkins came to the knowledge of Bournemouth detectives and, as there was nothing on her person to confirm identification other than a watch with the initials IMW on the back, notification was sent back to London. Her brother, Noel Wilkins, hurried to the scene, where he had the painful duty of identifying the body of his sister.

Although Irene was found lying on her back with her dress pulled up, Dr Harold Summons was able to inform detectives she had not been raped. A blunt instrument – probably a spanner – had caused the injuries to her head and she had also been punched in the face. Time of death was fixed at sometime before 8.20 p.m. Prior to this it had been raining and the top of her clothing was dry, while the parts in contact with the ground were soaked from the wet grass.

The police were also fortunate that the body had been found so early in the morning. The road beside the field was well used by locals; and at the spot close to where the body was found were footprints and signs that a struggle had taken place here, along with a deep set of tyre tracks in the muddy lane, which suggested the car had parked up for a time. Checks found that a car with Dunlop Magnum tyres had made the tracks.

News of the discovery of the body and the tyre tracks was reported in the local newspapers. One man reading it was Frank Humphris, who had returned home to Bournemouth on the same train as Irene Wilkins. On Christmas morning, while neighbours were unwrapping presents, he was at Bournemouth's main police station – where he was able to tell detectives he had seen a girl matching Irene's description carrying a small suitcase exit the station in front of him and that she had climbed into a chauffeur-driven grey car.

Enquiries were carried out at Bournemouth Central. Edward Nash, a signalman at the station recalled the chauffeur as he had been questioned by him about the arrival of the Waterloo train. Nash had told him it was running late but that he was waiting on the wrong platform and directed him to the correct one.

Officers were sent to question all chauffeurs in the area, one of whom was 36-year-old Thomas Henry Allaway, employed by businessman Arthur Sutton whose premises were on Clifton Road, Southbourne. Sutton was the father of the man living at Beechhurst, where the telegram sent from London had been posted. Allaway drove a green-grey 1914 model four-seater Mercedes car and a check on the tyres found it was fitted with three Dunlop Magnums and one Michelin tyre. However, from the position of the tyre imprints it was clear the Michelin was on the wrong wheel to match the tracks in the field.

Allaway denied changing any of the tyres recently, and when officers spoke to his employer they learned the Mercedes was locked up in a garage at Haviland Road at the time Irene Wilkins was seen climbing into a car. As Sutton had the only key this supported Allaway's alibi that he was drinking in the Salisbury Hotel, a local public house.

Detectives focussed on the telegram sent to Streatham and interviewed Alice Waters, the postal clerk at Bournemouth. She had spoken to the man sending it and had questioned him about the address. She said she would probably recognise him if she saw him again and heard him speak. Garrett also learned that over the previous week two other telegrams had been returned and examining them he noticed they appeared to have been written in the same handwriting and each contained spelling mistakes. Another clerk, Lillian Diplock, based at Boscombe from where one telegram had been sent also recalled the sender and felt sure she would recognise him again.

Detectives then heard from a nurse who had replied to a telegram, and had also made the trip to Bournemouth on the 4.30 p.m. Waterloo train, but had missed her stop. By the time she reached the station there had been no car waiting when she arrived and the taxi she summoned was unable to direct her to the address on the telegram. Unaware at the time of her lucky escape, she had cursed and returned home.

On 31 December Irene's attaché case was discovered in a wood at Branksome near Poole and five days later, on 4 January 1922, two weeks after the murder, Frank Humphris again spotted the car he had seen Irene getting in to. Now aware of its significance in relation to the murder enquiry, he noted the registration number – LK 7405 – and reported it to the police. However, possibly due to the amount of enquiries being undertaken – over 22,000 papers were eventually received – officers failed to follow up his report.

The Mercedes driven by chauffer Thomas Allaway. (Author's Collection)

A month later Lillian Diplock recognised a uniformed chauffer sending a telegram as the same man detectives wished to interview. She told a fellow clerk and hurried after him but by the time they could get to the door, the man had vanished. A few weeks later she heard the voice again. This time she managed to see the man standing beside a grey–green Mercedes. She took its number – LK 7405 – and reported it to the police. Again officers failed to follow up the lead. Days later the chauffeur was seen again by Miss Diplock. Again she told one of her fellow workers, and this time the man was followed to an address in Portman Mews. It was the home of Mr and Mrs Sutton and, as before, the police took no action.

In April, Allaway, perhaps aware that the search for the chauffer, which was constantly in the local papers, was going to lead back to him, ended his employment with Mr Sutton, but not before taking his chequebook with him. Forging a number of cheques he obtained over £20, which he used to take his wife and young daughter away from Hampshire.

Eventually, detectives sifting through the evidence came across the witness statements relating to the Mercedes and decided it was time they interviewed Allaway. Finding he had fled, they launched a nationwide hunt for him which eventually led officers to Reading. They discovered where Allaway was living and a constable was posted to keep watch.

On the evening of 28 April Thomas Allaway was spotted as he approached the house, but seeing a policeman he turned on his heels. The bobby was no longer a young man and the combination of his age and portly frame meant that the suspect was soon

Above left: *Thomas Allaway. (T.J. Leech Archive)*

Above right: *Allaway in the dock. (Author's Collection)*

able to outrun him. Fortunately for the officer, a member of the public was alerted to the shouts of 'stop that man' and stuck out a foot as Allaway passed, sending him sprawling to the ground. Before he could get to his feet the officer was able to rest his ample frame on his prisoner and hold him until assistance arrived. Taken into custody, Allaway was found to have a number of betting slips in his pocket, the handwriting on which matched that on the telegram sent to Irene Wilkins.

The tyres on Sutton's Mercedes were closely examined again; the Michelin, which had been enough to discount the car from initial enquiries, was found to be more worn than the others on the car and a check on the spare found that it was a Dunlop Magnum matching the others on the car and, more importantly, matching the tell-tale marks left at the scene of the murder. A witness was then found who had seen Allaway changing the tyre after the murder had taken place.

In order to break Allaway's alibi detectives needed to show that despite Sutton's statement that the car had been in the garage at 7 p.m. on that Friday night, it had been in the possession of Allaway.

A search of his old lodgings unearthed a key and, when checked, it fitted Sutton's lock-up garage. Allaway later admitted he had copied the key, allowing him to take the car whenever he chose.

When Allaway stood trial before Mr Justice Avory at Winchester Assizes in July the prosecution had a strong case. Both postal clerks had picked Allaway out of an identity parade, and his handwriting, found on the betting slips and on bundles of letters he had written to his wife while serving in the Royal Army Service Corps during the First World War, matched those on the telegrams.

Outlining their case, prosecution counsel Thomas W.H. Inskip KC said that Allaway had lured his victim to Bournemouth for the purpose of carrying out a sexual assault. Witnesses had been found who had seen the prisoner buying a copy of the *Morning Post* on the day Irene Wilkins's advertisement appeared; the postal clerk identified Allaway as the man who had sent the telegram and Frank Humphris testified he was the man driving the car which had met Irene Wilkins at the station.

Most damning was the handwriting on the three telegrams, which experts proved had both been written and sent by the prisoner. All the telegrams contained spelling mistakes: the same mistakes Allaway made when he was asked to write out some of the words they contained.

Defence counsel Mr A.C. Fox-Davies KC told the court that the accused had an alibi. He said that Allaway had finished his duties in the early evening and had gone out at 6.30 p.m; he had spent the night in a public house and, as he did not have access to the locked garage, he could not have possibly taken the car.

Mr Justice Avory, with black cap on his wig, captured sentencing Allaway to death. (Author's Collection)

LPC4 recording that Allaway had died of asphyxia. (Author's Collection)

Note by prison officials following the second botched execution. (Author's Collection)

The alibi was effectively shattered when the duplicate key was produced, along with a witness who claimed to have seen the prisoner at the Haviland Road garage three times on the night of the murder (and who declared that the car had been taken out of the garage before 7 p.m).

Allaway performed badly in the witness box: he stumbled through some of the questions put to him and when he was eventually returned to the dock there were few in the court who believed any other verdict than guilty as charged would be returned. On the fifth day of the trial, 7 July, the jury heard Mr Justice Avory sum up for over two hours before being invited to consider their verdict. Exactly one hour after retiring they returned to find Allaway guilty of murder.

A press photographer concealing a camera was able to record the moment the black cap was draped onto the judge's wig; the prisoner stood emotionless in the dock as he was condemned to death. An appeal, which heard evidence that new witnesses had come forward to support Allaway's alibi, was quickly dismissed and he was returned to Winchester to await the hangman.

Allaway confessed his guilt to the prison governor on the night before he was led to the gallows. Due to a recent fire that had destroyed the chapel, no bell was tolled as the procession reached the scaffold. There Ellis placed the noose around Allaway's neck and then pulled the lever. It seemed, as with the previous execution at the gaol, Ellis had failed to line up the prisoner's feet in the centre of the drop, for as Allaway's body fell through the trap it lurched to one side, slamming into the edge of the drop and shifting the position of the knot. Allaway died due to asphyxiation rather than of a broken neck as planned. As this was a repeat of what had happened at the previous execution an enquiry was launched: this found that the trapdoors at Winchester were much smaller than at other gaols. As a result new gallows was constructed at the end of D wing.

22

FOR THE MONEY

St Lucia Barracks was one of many army camps that littered the Surrey and Hampshire countryside. To serve the large number of military personnel, many of the city banks opened small branches close to these sites which would be staffed on one or two days a week. The Lloyd's Bank branch at Bordon Camp was a typical example of a small hut sited close to an army base and served by one clerk, who would make weekly visits to see the banking needs of the camp and to process the soldiers' pay.

It was fast approaching three o'clock on the afternoon of Thursday 3 April 1924, when Sam Brooker, a clerk employed by the Midland Bank, looked at his watch and began to worry that something was wrong. The bus that would take him and his friend, 29-year-old William Edward Hall, the clerk at Lloyd's, back to their home at Farnham was due any minute and there was no sign of Mr Hall. The men had similar jobs, travelling to the various branches of their respective banks on separate days of the week, and as both visited Bordon on Thursdays they would travel to and from the camp on the same bus.

Brooker knew that Hall would close his branch at 2 p.m. and then tend to any paperwork before locking up and walking to the bus stop in good time for the 3.05 p.m. bus. Worried that something may be amiss, Brooker walked back to the hut and found it closed. Returning to the bus stop he spoke to Harry Payne, the local postman, who knew both clerks well. 'Mr Hall hasn't turned up for the bus and his hut is closed,' he said. 'I wonder where he could have got to?'

Both returned to the branch and, walking around the back of the hut, they peered through a small window. 'Good God!' Payne cried, as he spotted what appeared to be a bullet hole in the glass. They forced the window and found the body of William Hall in a pool of blood behind the counter. The police were called and PC Francis Gay was the first to reach the bank. He summoned assistance and detectives, in the company of Alton-based pathologist Dr Henry Williams, were soon on the scene. Williams was able to confirm that death was due to wounds from a gun fired at close quarters. One bullet had entered the neck and exited through the back of the skull; the other was still in the head. The bullet was a .45 calibre fired from a Webley service revolver. Death would have been instantaneous.

Lloyds Bank at Bordon Camp. (Author's Collection)

William Hall's body lying behind the counter. (TNA PRO)

The trajectory of the bullet suggested to detectives that the weapon had been fired from the public side of the counter, and the likely cause was robbery as over £1,000 in treasury notes was missing. The officer assigned to the case was Superintendent Walter Jones of the Hampshire Constabulary. His first task was to make a series of test shots to gauge the noise level outside the bank. They found that the shots were inaudible in the nearest building, the post office, but even if the postmaster had heard shots at the time of the murder it would hardly have warranted a second thought as the branch was next to an army camp, which sported a number of rifle ranges.

The first lead the officers had to pursue was the repeated sighting of a small red motorcar, which several people mentioned as being seen in the vicinity around the time of the attack. A postmaster claimed to have spotted a car with its engine revving outside the bank at 2.30 p.m., and various other witnesses claimed to have seen it cruising around on the previous day. Detectives made strenuous efforts to trace the car but it was to no avail.

Inquiries were also centred on the soldiers based at Bordon Camp. St Lucia barracks was the home of the 2nd East Lancashire Regiment and Superintendent Jones was faced with the daunting task of determining the movements of the 6,000 soldiers.

One name quickly cropped up as a likely suspect. L-Cpl Abraham 'Jack' Goldenberg was mentioned as one of the men who had business at the bank on that afternoon. When interviewed, Goldenberg admitted he had cashed a cheque at the bank at 1.45 p.m., and that he was the only customer there at the time. Detectives discovered that he was a 22-year-old Jew, a native of South Wales, who was engaged to a girl who didn't practice the Jewish faith. As a result his father, living at the family home in Manchester, strongly disapproved of his relationship with a 'Shicksa' – a Gentile girl.

They also learned that Goldenberg needed money. Three weeks before the murder he had seen the camp commander and asked for a discharge so that he could marry and take up a position as a clerk in his fiancée's home town of Preston, Lancashire, where he had been stationed before the company moved south to Bordon Camp. Goldenberg was told he could only leave if he bought himself out of the army and unless he could afford the £35 to secure his release, he must see out the rest of his time. This clearly upset him but he seemed to reluctantly resign himself to army life for the immediate future.

Late in the afternoon of Tuesday 8 April, Goldenberg left the camp to post a letter to his girl. Returning to the camp he was spotted by Sgt-Maj. Alliott. He was suspicious of the reclusive soldier and had ordered a soldier in the regimental band to keep an eye out for him. The bandsman watched as Goldenberg entered a latrine and reach up into the rafters for a package. Seeing Goldenberg pull out a handful of notes, he quickly fetched the sergeant-major. Goldenberg was caught red-handed with the stolen money and placed in the guardroom. As the arrest was taking place, William Hall was being buried in his native Swansea, which, by a strange quirk of fate, was also the birthplace of Goldenberg.

Superintendent Jones rushed to the camp and charged the young soldier with murder. Goldenberg broke down and readily told them where they would find the stolen money, although he was insistent that the £37 found in his wallet was his own.

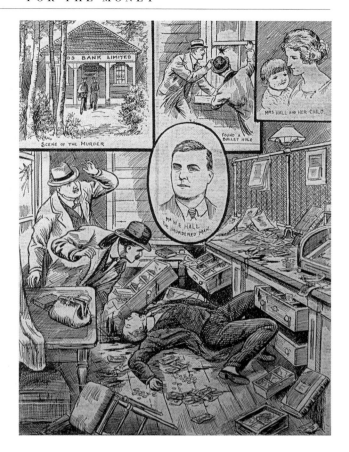

The Illustrated Police News
records the murder of William
Hall. (T.J. Leech Archive)

A search of the camp yielded the rest of the haul and they found the murder weapon, a
Webley revolver, which had been stolen from the camp stores at the end of March and
buried in a wood close-by.

On 11 April, three days after his arrest, he made a confession in which he blamed
an accomplice for the actual murder. Goldenberg alleged a man named Meredith had
entered the hut while he had kept lookout. He claimed they had decided to rob the bank,
but had agreed there would be no violence. Goldenberg claimed Meredith had rushed
from the hut and from the look on his face he sensed something was wrong. Entering the
bank, he found Hall lying dead and, realising his predicament, he locked the place up
and concealed the money until he could think of what to do with it. Goldenberg claimed
he had not reported it earlier as he didn't want to 'split' on his friend.

When he appeared in court following his arrest, Goldenberg looked a broken man.
The stripe he had proudly sported on the arm of his tunic had been ripped off, as had
his shoulder flashes. He was unwashed, dazed and appeared to have been crying as he
was led into the dock. Evidence was heard regarding the crime and the short sitting
ended with a further remand. There were to be several more hearings before he was
finally committed for trial.

Abraham 'Jack' Goldenberg.
(Author's Collection)

The money was hidden in the latrines at the camp.
(TNA PRO)

Abraham Goldenberg was tried at Winchester Assizes on 19 June 1924, before Mr Justice Bailhache. Mr Holman Gregory KC led for the Crown, and stated that the prosecution's case was that 'the murder had been deliberately planned by a Jew who had turned Gentile, to obtain money to marry a Gentile girl.'

The defence, led by Mr Ernest Hancock KC, claimed they could prove their client's innocence and pointed to the prisoner meeting a sailor called Meredith before the murder, and produced an anonymous letter it claimed they had received. Initialled 'M' and postmarked London E1, dated 12.15 p.m., 17 June 1924, it read:

Sir. I understand that Abraham Goldenberg, at present in Winchester Prison, charged with murdering Hall, the Bordon bank manager, will be tried tomorrow. I want you to know he did not kill Hall. I shot, him, but it was only an accident. I am sorry I cannot come to you personally, as it is not convenient, but I hope you will not punish Goldenberg for what he did not do. The kid is a regular sport. I have sent the same letter to Goldenberg's solicitors and to the judge.

The prosecution quickly dismissed the letter as a hoax, claiming there was no evidence to support 'Meredith', or any third party, being involved in the murder. They referred to a confession made by the prisoner shortly after his arrest, in which he was alleged to have stated:

> I was as calm as I am now. The door was open and I just went in and said, 'Put your hands up!' He made for the drawer so I just gave him one, two and down he went. I got the keys and locked up the door. I got what I could, and got out of the bank. I have not the slightest regret for what I have done, but I am sorry for my girl and Mrs Hall. I needed the money because my girlfriend would not contemplate marriage until I was in a better financial position.

The statement ended with the chilling remark: 'I would do it again for the money.'

To most people in the crowded courtroom the prisoner's fate looked grim. The defence realised they had no chance of an acquittal and chose the only option open to them, and asked for a verdict of guilty but insane. Hancock said he would show that there was a history of insanity in Goldenberg's family.

The first defence witness was the prisoner's father, Solomon Goldenberg. As the sad old man entered the dock, Goldenberg rose from his chair and shouted 'dad!' The man looked across at his son and tears filled his eyes. He told the court how one of his daughters had been a frequent outpatient at an asylum, and his own sister had recently died in Bridgend Asylum, and at least eight members of the immediate family suffered from some kind of mental illness.

He concluded his evidence by claiming that the prisoner had injured his head in a fall and from then on had become a loner with a marked change in his persona. A number of personal letters written by the accused were read out, which showed he was paranoiac, particularly about the size of his nose. Goldenberg had been having treatment to have it reduced because he felt people were constantly laughing at him, and had even bought a machine which claimed it could reduce the size of his nose. The letters carried such lines as, 'I cannot stand it anymore,' and, 'life is simply a curse to me.'

The judge questioned the prisoner's father about his son's relationship with a Christian girl. He asked if it was true that he had had nothing to do with his son because of it, and the old man agreed. Mr Gregory asked if it was true his son was in love with a woman called Ada, but, before his father could answer, the prisoner jumped to his feet protesting at the reference to her name, shouting, 'Do not mention it, I would rather hang!'

The defence called Mr Devine, a Harley Street neurologist, who told the court he was of the opinion that the prisoner was suffering from a mental condition known as *dementia praecox*, a recurrent form of disease that renders a person incapable of judging the nature of an action he commits. Dr Norwood East, medical officer of HM prisons, was called by the prosecution and said he had examined the prisoner on a number of occasions before coming to the conclusion that Goldenberg was perfectly sane.

In his final summing up for the Crown, Mr Gregory said that Goldenberg had crossed over faith and become a Christian, had fallen in love with a Christian girl and when it became a question between his family and his girl, the girl won. He knew there was money in the bank and in order to secure his freedom from the army and marry his sweetheart he chose to commit robbery, which resulted in the murder of an innocent man.

The jury took only a short time to find the prisoner guilty as charged and he was sentenced to death. As the judge concluded passing sentence, Goldenberg spoke: 'Can I be assured the £37 found on me will be declared my property?' Clearly startled, the judge made no reply as the prisoner was ushered from the dock.

Following conviction Goldenberg reverted back to the Jewish faith and lodged an appeal but on 14 July it was rejected and he was returned to the condemned cell at Winchester Gaol.

On the morning of 30 July, Goldenberg was hanged by Tom Pierrepoint and assistant William Willis on a newly-constructed gallows at the end of D wing. He had made a boast from his cell that he intended to cheat the gallows, but the posting of extra guards in the condemned cell saw that he was prevented from carrying out his threat. Willis later noted in his diary that the condemned man had shown no nerves on the morning of his execution, swaggering to the gallows with his head held high as though savouring the final moment. As Pierrepoint adjusted the noose Goldenberg cried out, 'Father forgive me,' before the trap was sprung and he dropped to his death.

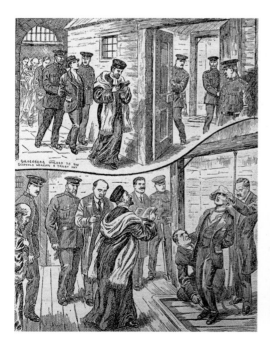

Above left: *Goldenberg's execution as featured in the* Illustrated Police News. *(T.J. Leech Archive)*

Above right: *Hangman Tom Pierrepoint. (Author's Collection)*

23

MURDERED FOR FIFTEEN SHILLINGS

Charles Edward Finden, 12 August 1926

With his wages of 15s in his pocket, 14-year-old John Richard Thompson finished work for the week as a garden boy employed by Capt. Cookson at Old Farm House, Beech, on the outskirts of Alton. Instead of heading straight home, he watched a cricket match in a local park before calling into a shop, where he ordered some poultry feed for Capt. Cookson, to be collected later, before heading towards a footpath beside Wyatt's Farm on Basingstoke Road that took him towards Flood Meadow (where he would often go bird nesting). When he failed to return home that night, Saturday 5 June 1926, his worried parents contacted the police and a hunt was set up.

Two gipsy boys, Jack Black and Arthur Cole had travelled to Alton to make arrangements for the burial of a baby belonging to one of their camp. The baby's sister had been buried in a cemetery here and, having gained permission for the interment, they set up camp in a nearby field in readiness for the arrival of the other travellers. On the following evening they were making their way back to the field close beside the Alton to Basingstoke railway line when they noticed a boy's cap lying on the ground, which had been trampled as if a struggle had taken place there. They then looked to see if the owner was nearby and found the body of the young boy half hidden in a hedge.

Superintendent Abel of the Hampshire Constabulary began a murder enquiry and the police surgeon, Dr Henry Williams, carried out a medical examination. He found that John Thompson had been strangled with his own necktie having been first struck in the face with what he believed was a heavy stick, fracturing the skull. The motive for the murder was clearly robbery as the 15s wages Thompson had in his possession after leaving work was missing and his pockets had been turned out.

Detectives piecing together the boy's last movements learned that after leaving the shop at 5 p.m., where he had ordered the chicken feed, Thompson had last been seen on the road leading to Basingstoke, in the company of a man. On the following afternoon, Charles Finden, a tall, slim, youthful-looking 22-year-old labourer with a mop of blond hair, who lived with his wife and young daughter at River View, Alton, was detained and interviewed as he matched the description of the wanted man.

Above: *Charles Finden. (T.J. Leech Archive)*

Right: *A news-cutting featuring the 'Alton Murder'. (Author's Collection)*

BOY'S HAT NEAR HEDGE.

Grim Discovery by Gipsies.

COINCIDENCE IN ERRAND OF MERCY.

TWO gipsy boys, John Black and Arthur Cole, went to Alton, Hampshire, to make arrangements for the burial of a baby belonging to their travelling band. The child's sister had been buried there, and when they had obtained permission for the little one to be placed in a neighbouring grave they went into the fields on the outskirts of the town and made a temporary camp.

Returning to the town, where they proposed to spend the evening, they saw a boy's cap lying in the field near the railway line, and searching for the owner discovered the body of a boy lying half-hidden in a hedge.

The ground had been trampled as in a struggle, and the boy's own tie had been tightly knotted round his neck. There was a wound in the head. The body was that of John Richard Thompson, aged 14, the son of a carter in Lenten-road, Alton, who for some time had been garden boy employed by Capt. Cookson, R.N., at Old Farm, Beech, outside Alton, at 18s. a week. Thompson was paid his wages at 4 o'clock in the afternoon, and was seen among the spectators at a cricket match until about five o'clock.

John Thompson.

Finden had recently been working as a platelayer and labourer with the Southern Railway until he lost his job following a strike, and he had previously served in the King's Royal Rifles, ending his service with an exemplary character reference. He matched the description a number of witnesses had given of the man seen walking with the boy late on Saturday afternoon and when put up in an identification parade several people picked him out as the man seen in the company of John Thompson. Finden was questioned about his movements on the Saturday evening and while he admitted being in the vicinity of where the boy had been found murdered, and that he knew the boy well enough to speak to, he said that he had fallen asleep in Flood Meadows and had been there from 2.30 p.m. until around 6.15 p.m.

Finden's wife told detectives that on Saturday evening her husband had given her some money which he said he had earned by doing some labouring work on the nearby tennis courts. Asked how much, she said it was 15s, in the form of two half crowns and a ten-shilling note. Detectives had already learned from Capt. Cookson that he had paid Thompson's wages with a ten-shilling note and two half crowns and when enquiries at the tennis club failed to substantiate Finden's alibi he was charged with murder. Finden then changed his story and said the money he had given his wife had been unemployment benefit, but it was felt too much of a coincidence.

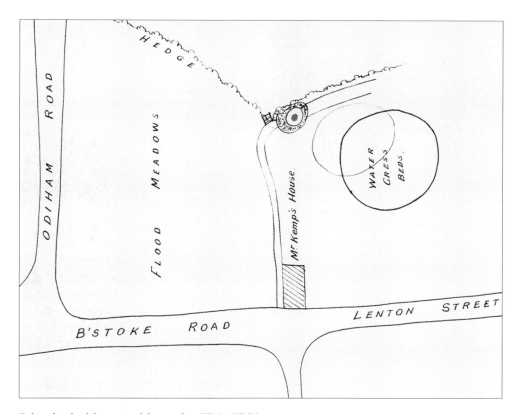

Police sketch of the scene of the murder. (TNA PRO)

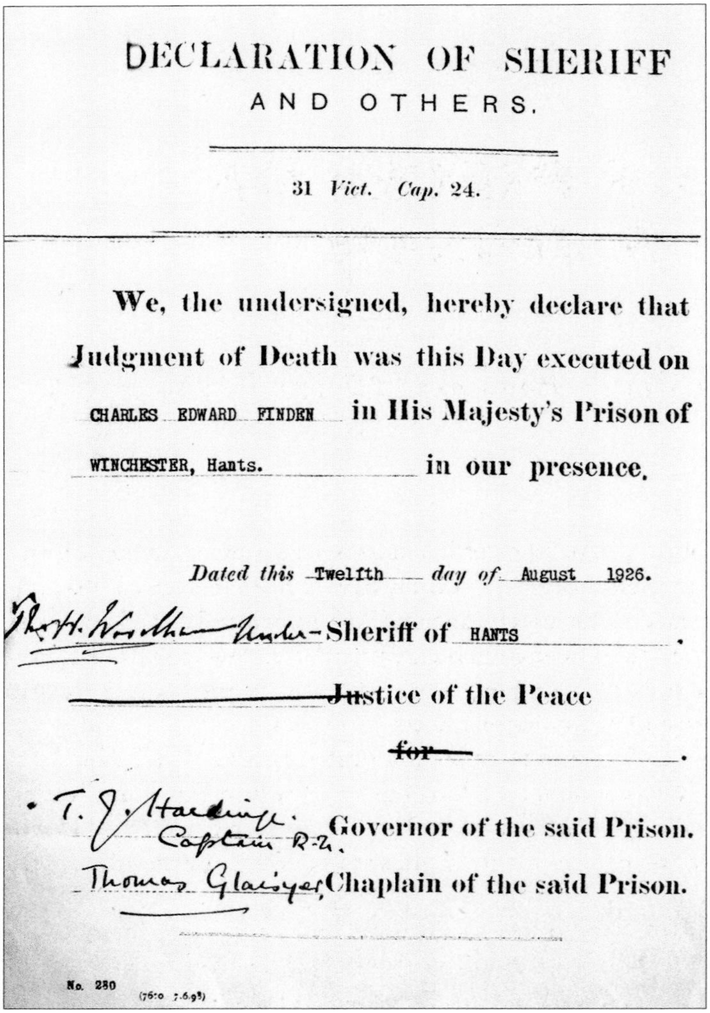

DECLARATION OF SHERIFF
AND OTHERS.

31 *Vict.* *Cap.* 24.

We, the undersigned, hereby declare that
Judgment of Death was this Day executed on
CHARLES EDWARD FINDEN   in His Majesty's Prison of
WINCHESTER, Hants.   in our presence.

Dated this Twelfth   day of August   1926.

[signature] Under-Sheriff of HANTS   .

                    Justice of the Peace

                    for

• *T. J. Hardinge*
   Captain R.N.   Governor of the said Prison.

Thomas Glaisyer, Chaplain of the said Prison.

No. 230   (76:0 7.6.93)

*Notice of Finden's
execution. (Author's
Collection)*

He stood trial before Mr Justice Roche on 5 July at Winchester Assizes and pleaded
not guilty. The prosecution built a strong case of circumstantial evidence, mainly the
money he had given to his wife and the identification made by people who had seen
him in the company of the boy prior to the murder. After an absence of forty minutes,
the jury returned to find Finden guilty and his wife's hysterical sobbing rang around the
sombre courtroom as sentence of death was passed.

Finden penned numerous letters to his wife and blamed the prison authorities for
restricting the amount of paper he was allowed – otherwise, he told his wife, he would
have written much longer letters. One of his final letters, in which he maintained his
innocence, said that he was not afraid of what the future held: 'I am ready to go if I
have got to, and I only hope my mother will be there to meet me. I shall not be afraid
to meet young Thompson, for he knows I am innocent!'

24

LIKE PIECES OF A JIGSAW

William Henry Podmore, 22 April 1930

After successfully running a number of businesses in America, including the construction of a tunnel under the Hudson River, much-travelled 58-year-old Vivian Messiter returned to his native England in September 1928. Something of an enigma, Messiter was quiet, uncommunicative and with few friends, the one-time student of medicine switched to engineering, and he was commissioned into the Northumberland Fusiliers, ending his military career as a captain.

Messiter had returned to England to take up a post with the Wolf's Head Oil Company based in Southampton and took lodgings at 3 Carlton Road, in the city. Messiter acted as an agent for the oil company and after securing premises at 42 Grove Street, he placed an advertisement in the local press at the end of the month for sub-agents to work for him.

On Tuesday morning, 30 October, he rose at dawn and took an early breakfast, telling his landlord, Albert Parrott, a former policeman, that he had an urgent appointment. He was never seen alive again. Two days later, Parrott called to the garage on Grove Street but found all the doors were locked and there was no sign of Vivian Messiter. The landlord had already surmised from conversations with Messiter that business was struggling, and when he failed to return home that night (or on the following day), he assumed he had simply done a 'flit' and walked away from the business.

Two months passed and with still no word from their southern area agent, officers of the Wolf's Head headquarters appointed a new agent, a Mr Passmore. On 10 January 1929 Passmore went to Grove Street to start work. With no keys to the heavy padlock securing the garage he needed assistance to force entry and once inside he surveyed his new premises. He was soon attracted to a strange smell coming from behind some oil-drums and when he made his way across the storeroom the mystery of the disappearance of Vivian Messiter was solved and a murder hunt was about to begin.

At first glance it appeared that Messiter had been shot in the head. Local police called in Scotland Yard and Detective Chief Inspector John Prothero arrived in Southampton to lead the enquiry. Prothero immediately requested the assistance of Dr

Bernard Spilsbury and he was soon able to tell detectives that Messiter had not been shot: instead he been battered to death, presumably with the hammer found beside the body. A detailed search of the storeroom revealed two scraps of paper, one being a note from Messiter to a Mr W.F. Thomas, and when Messiter's lodgings were searched, a letter, a reply to the advertisement Messiter had placed, was discovered also bearing the name William F. Thomas with an address of 5 Cranberry Avenue, Southampton.

When officers visited Cranberry Avenue they found that Thomas had already moved on and had left a forwarding address that turned out to be false. The details they already had on Thomas were circulated to other forces and soon brought interesting results. Police in Wiltshire informed Prothero that they were looking for Thomas in connection with the theft of some wage packets from a garage at Downton, near Salisbury on 21 December.

Thomas had disappeared from his lodgings, which were checked by detectives in Wiltshire, and another scrap of paper was found, this time bearing the name Podmore with an address in Manchester. They were now able to determine that William F. Thomas was in fact an alias for one William Henry Podmore, a man known to police in Manchester where he was wanted on a charge of fraud.

Above left: *Vivian Messiter.* (*Author's Collection*)

Above right: *The garage on Grove Street Southampton.* (*Author's Collection*)

Above left: *The murder weapon. (Author's Collection)*

Above right: *Det. Chief Insp. John Prothero (centre) going over evidence with fellow detectives. (Author's Collection)*

The next lead came from Stoke-on-Trent. Police officers there also had an interest in Podmore and could supply more information. He was known to spend time with a woman named Lily Hambleton, who the press dubbed 'Golden Haired Lil', and on 17 January, she was traced and questioned at her home. She told detectives that she and Podmore often stayed at the Leicester Hotel on Vauxhall Bridge Road, London, and when officers visited this address they caught up with William Henry Podmore.

Although he was strongly suspected as being the man wanted for the murder of Vivian Messiter, Prothero as yet had insufficient evidence to charge him, so he bided his time as Podmore was transferred to Manchester to face the charges of fraud. He was sentenced to three months and on his release he was immediately re-arrested and transferred to Winchester where he received a further six months sentence for theft at Downton.

All the while the Scotland Yard men were slowly building their case on the charge of murder and a breakthrough came when Prothero closely examined the receipt book for oil-sale commissions. He noticed that there was an indentation on one of the pages from the page above, which had been torn out, and was able to show that they were

William Henry Podmore.
(Author's Collection)

for a sale dated 28 October, two days before Messiter disappeared. The receipt was signed 'WFT' and suggested that Podmore, using the alias Thomas, had been claiming commission for bogus sales and he had removed the incriminating page in the hope of avoiding detection. 'Why else would anyone remove the page unless they were trying to conceal a crime?' Prothero pondered with his team.

Prothero's case was built upon the belief that when he learnt of the swindling Messiter had confronted Podmore; being aware of the Manchester charge and the likelihood of imprisonment if it went further, he had panicked, lost his nerve and murdered Messiter by striking him with the hammer.

When he heard he was to be tried at Winchester Assizes, Podmore was so confident of being acquitted that he boasted to fellow inmates: 'The old farmers in Hampshire don't know how to try a man.' In due course he appeared before Lord Chief Justice Gordon Hewart on 8 March, where during a six-day trial all the evidence Prothero had gathered – like pieces of the jigsaw – fitted perfectly together to built an overwhelming case against the accused. Following a summing up by Hewart, heavily biased against the prisoner, the jury convicted Podmore in just eighty-three minutes and he was sentenced to death.

25

A FAREWELL KISS

Sidney Archibald Frederick Chamberlain, 28 July 1949

Although he was married with a wife living at home at Ellis Place, Heavitree, Exeter, lorry driver Sidney Chamberlain had been having a relationship with Doreen Messenger, ever since they had met during a visit to his sister's house, and they had carried on the illicit affair until her family found out. Despite the infidelity, which Doreen's parents most definitely did not approve of, they were even more concerned about the age difference between the couple. At 31 years old, Chamberlain was over twice the age of his 15-year-old girlfriend and they were told to stop the relationship. There were a number of arguments at her family home in Meadow Way, Heavitree, and to appease her parents Doreen agreed to end the affair.

They parted for a short time but then secretly started seeing each again, and on Friday evening, 18 February 1949, Doreen finished work for the day and collected her wages of 1s 6d. Chamberlain picked her up in his car and they drove out into the moors near Chudleigh. They spent the night kissing and cuddling in the car while discussing their future together. Both knew the relationship was doomed and both were upset at the situation they had found themselves in, especially as his wife had now discovered the affair and made it clear that it had to end.

At lunchtime on the following afternoon a man out walking on the moor noticed what he thought was a pile of rags. On closer inspection he found it was the body of a young girl, naked except for a pair of stockings and covered with an overcoat and a pair of overalls. Police officers investigating what was clearly a case of murder already had a likely identity for the victim as Doreen's parents had reported her as missing to the police when she had failed to return home on the previous evening. A post-mortem, carried out by Dr George Lynch at Torbay Hospital, found that cause of death was manual strangulation and, although there was evidence of intimacy having taken place, there was no sign of pregnancy.

They also had a name of a potential suspect – Sidney Chamberlain – and when detectives went to his house they found that he had vanished. A search for the killer began but it was a manhunt of a different kind that was to lead to Chamberlain's arrest. Across the county police officers were on the lookout for an escaped prisoner,

Sidney Chamberlain's car. (TNA PRO)

on the run after absconding from Dartmoor Gaol, and as a result roadblocks set up in many places, stopping cars and questioning drivers and their passengers. That Saturday night a roadblock was in place on the main Exeter to Plymouth road near Newton Abbot when Chamberlain's car approached. Instead of heeding the request to stop, Chamberlain hit the accelerator and raced away, quickly pursued by a police motorcyclist.

The pursuit lasted just a short time as Chamberlain drove off the road and crashed his car into a grass bank. He gave the officer his name and, taken to a police station at Plymouth, he was searched and found to be carrying a pair of scissors. Detectives already knew that Doreen's killer had cut her clothes with a pair of scissors, but on being questioned Chamberlain claimed to know nothing about the murder.

Taken to the cells, he told a detective that he had 'laid her out after she had died.' He later made a statement in which he claimed they had met up after Doreen had finished work and drove to Teignmouth with the intention of going to the pictures. He said that Doreen had then changed her mind so they drove up to Haldon Moor near Chudleigh and parked the car in what he called their 'special place.'

Here, they had talked about the difficulties they were having and as he kissed her, she started to cry, telling him she would rather be dead than leave him. Chamberlain said he told her he felt the same and they had remained on the moor until it was almost dawn, by which time Doreen said she would get a good hiding when she got home. She told him she didn't want to go home and at that Chamberlain said he put his hands around Doreen's throat.

He said that he began to squeeze and after some moments her body began to shudder. Chamberlain said he had stopped and asked Doreen if she was all right. She did not reply, but leaned forward and kissed him. He said he had then continued to apply pressure to her throat until she slumped into unconsciousness. Chamberlain then claimed that as she was still breathing he took off his belt and continued strangling her with it. When she was finally dead, Chamberlain dragged her body from the car out onto the moor, where he then removed her clothing, cutting parts of them with the scissors, until she was almost totally naked. He then claimed to have had sex with the dead body.

Chamberlain was tried at Exeter Assizes held in Exeter Castle. The trial began on 16 June before Mr Justice Jones with J.D. Casswell KC leading for the crown and Henry Elam handling the case for the defence. Casswell claimed that Chamberlain, having become tired of Doreen and with the strain of keeping the relationship a secret, had deliberately murdered her, and his statement made following his arrest was a detailed confession to a brutal murder.

SHE DIDN'T KNOW OF KISS—SHE WAS DEAD Alleged statement

THE story of a farewell kiss was told at Devon Assizes yesterday when Sidney Archibald Frederick Chamberlain, 31, pleaded not guilty of murdering Doreen Primrose Messenger, 15, whose body was found on Haldon Moor, near Chudleigh, on February 19.

Mr. J. D. Casswell, K.C., opening the case, said the defence would be one of insanity. He said that Chamberlain made a statement that on the evening of February 18 he drove Doreen into he country as he usually did.

"We got into the back of the car and we were kissing each other. She said that rather than leave me she would rather be dead." the statement went on.

"We stayed cuddling

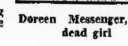

Doreen Messenger, the dead girl

Newspaper cutting detailing Doreen's murder. (Author's Collection)

Left: A policeman marks the spot where Doreen Messenger's body was found. (TNA PRO)

Below: A letter advising assistant executioner Harry Allen of preliminary arrangements regarding Chamberlain's execution. (Author's Collection)

All communications should be addressed to "The Governor" and not to any official by name.

H. M. PRISON,

Winchester,Hants.

22nd June 1949.

Dear Sir,

Sidney Archibald Frederick Chamberlain.

With reference to the execution of the above named, which has been fixed by the Under Sheriff of Devon to take place at this establishment on 5th July 1949, I have been forwarded your name as one competent to act as Assistant Executioner.

I attach hereto Memorandum of Conditions attending this post.

Should the date of execution be changed you will immediately be notified by letter.

Yours faithfully,

Governor.

Mr. H.B.Allen,
Rawson Arms Hotel,
Peel Street,
Farnworth, Bolton, Lancs.

Above left: *Details of Chamberlain's execution from the assistant hangman's diary. (Author's Collection)*

Above right: *Albert Pierrepoint. (Author's Collection)*

His defence was insanity and Elam told the court that Chamberlain had a mental age of 11. Neurologist Dr Paul Sandifer, called by the defence, described how Chamberlain had shown psychopathic tendencies and that he had smiled as he told the story of how he had had sex with Doreen's body. Chamberlain's sister testified that when she was 8 years old, her brother had stabbed her under the left eye with some scissors. As a result, she was blind in that eye.

The judge told the jury of ten men and two women in his summing up that having a low mental age is not the same as being insane. The trial lasted two days and the jury took just thirty minutes to decide that Chamberlain was guilty and sane. Following an unsuccessful appeal Chamberlain became the first man to go to the gallows at Winchester in almost twenty years.

26

SHOT DOWN IN THE STREET

Zbigniew Gower & Roman Redel, 7 July 1950

It looked an easy target. From their seat on the upper deck of the bus making its way along North View, Durdham Down, Bristol, their attention was drawn to a small branch of Lloyds Bank. Further reconnaissance revealed that the branch comprised of a staff of just a single cashier and an elderly security guard. In their minds all they had to do was wave the gun and they would hand over the money. Then they would hop on the motorcycle stolen before the robbery and flee the scene. It seemed as simple and straightforward as that: in reality it turned out very different.

Zbigniew Gower and Roman Redel had arrived in Bristol from their native Poland at the end of the war. Either unable or unwilling to find regular employment both were out of work and short of money when they came up with the scheme to rob the bank. On Monday morning, 13 March 1950 they set about putting their plan into action. On the night before, to bolster their courage, they began to drink. And drink they did! The two men drank late into the night and consumed so much alcohol that on the morning of the robbery both were nursing dreadful hangovers. As a result, they had to abandon plans to steal the motorbike and instead made their way to the bank by bus.

Entering the small branch Redel marched straight to the counter and pulled out a gun while his companion vaulted the counter. Although cashier Ronald Wall, and the guard, retired police officer John Bullock, offered no resistance as Redel pointed the pistol at them and motioned them towards the side office, Gower was in a panic. From behind the counter he looked around for anyone entering through the front door and for any signs of a disturxbance in the office.

The raid lasted just a matter of seconds. Gower, not fully paying attention to what he was doing, pulled open the drawers snatching up the contents: a collection of paying-in slips and just £28 in cash. Fleeing the bank, the two Poles boarded a bus just about to depart from the adjacent stop. Had they made any attempt to tie up or lock the staff in the office they may have made good their getaway. Instead, once the robbers had exited, Bullock rushed from the bank and saw them board the bus. As it pulled away from the kerb he stood in front of it with his arms spread, imploring the driver to halt.

'Stop! Bandits on your bus!' he called out.

As the driver slammed on the brakes the two robbers jumped from their seats and made their way down from the upper deck. Bullock boarded the bus and found himself face-to-face with the two men. For the second time within minutes he found himself looking down the barrel of Redel's gun. The Pole shouted for him to get out of the way and both Redel and Gower jumped off and made their way up the pavement.

The guard, past retirement age, was unable to give chase but several passengers on the bus and a number of passers-by began to pursue the fleeing men. Taking the lead was 30-year-old Robert John 'Bob' Taylor of Fishponds, Bristol. Taylor, a keep-fit fanatic, judo expert and treasurer of the Bristol ju-jitsu club soon caught up with the Poles and attempted to make a citizen's arrest. Redel, the first to be detained, began to struggle with him. A shot rang out and Bob Taylor fell to the ground, a bullet in his head. Up ahead on the road Gower watched in horror as his friend left the man lying in a pool of blood and joined him in making their escape. Both were picked up within an hour and held on a charge of robbery and attempted murder which was subsequently changed to murder when Taylor died from his wounds later that morning.

Tried together at Salisbury Assizes by Mr Justice Oliver on 23 May, both made a passionate plea from the dock claiming to be innocent of the murder. Redel infuriated the judge by laughing as he told the court how both men getting drunk on the night before the robbery had ruined their planning. Whatever he may have testified there

Lloyd's Bank at Durdham Down, Bristol. (TNA PRO)

JUDO MAN SHOT—TWO ON MURDER CHARGE

Express Staff Reporter

ROBERT GEORGE TAYLOR, 29-year-old judo expert, who was shot dead in a Bristol street yesterday, is believed to have been trying to put a jiu-jitsu hold on two men after a hold-up at a local bank.

The North View branch of Lloyds Bank at Westbury had just opened when two men came in.

The cashier, Mr. R. F. Watt, and the bank guard, J. F. Bullock, were told, "This is a stick-up."

One man jumped the counter and snatched notes from the till. Both men ran out of the bank and jumped on a bus.

The conductor, 27-year-old Dennis Pellin, heard shouts of "Stop these men," and stopped the bus.

The men jumped off and Bank Guard Bullock was joined in the chase by shoppers.

They saw Robert Taylor, a grey-suited figure, narrow the gap at every stride to intercept the men. There was a shot, and he fell dead.

Taylor, who was single, was treasurer of the Bristol Judo Club.

Last night Roman Redel and Zbigniew Gower, both aged 23, were jointly charged with murdering Taylor, and will appear in court today.

ROBERT GEORGE TAYLOR . . . A grey-suited figure narrowed the gap at every stride.

Have-a-go hero Bob Taylor. (Author's Collection)

The two condemned cells on D wing where Gower and Redel awaited execution. (Alan Constable)

was never any doubt that Redel had actually fired the shot and was guilty of wilful murder. Gower, some way ahead of Redel during the chase when the shot was fired, fought desperately to save his own skin. He claimed he had no idea that Redel was carrying a gun, let alone that he would use it. He also tried to show that the planning and robbery were all Redel's doing, but it was shown in court that both were engaged in a common purpose – and therefore, by law, were equally as guilty.

After considering their verdict for just a short time, the jury returned to find both Redel and Gower guilty of murder, but in the case of Gower they gave a strong recommendation to mercy. As it was there would be no reprieve for either man. Redel, married with a wife of just 17, seemed to have accepted the inevitable, while the authorities suspected that Gower, believing he was suffering a miscarriage of justice, would put up a fight for his life.

Redel and Gower were hanged side by side by Albert Pierrepoint and three assistants. For assistant hangman Syd Dernley, who had broken off a family holiday to officiate at his seventh engagement, it would be a memorable execution. On arriving at their quarters, once the hangmen had prepared the scaffold for the following morning, Pierrepoint had launched into an angry tirade when the warder brought them their tea. Viewing the meal of ham and cress salad, which was balanced more in favour of the latter than the former, Pierrepoint called out angrily: 'What's this? We're not

Hangman Albert Pierrepoint and assistant Syd Dernley. (Author's Collection)

eating this muck... we want summat better than this...' The cook, who had gone home for the day, was summoned and a new meal of bacon and eggs was prepared for the executioners.

On the morning of the execution there would be another notable memory for assistant Dernley. Dernley was detailed to assist Pierrepoint in getting Redel onto the drop, with Harry Kirk and Herbert Allen given the job of escorting Gower. Believing Gower was the more likely to cause a scene he was positioned closest to the scaffold and Kirk and Allen had him pinioned and noosed as Pierrepoint and Dernley led Redel from the further condemned cell onto the drop. They reached the scaffold as Gower stood already noosed and waiting, and as Pierrepoint positioned the rope Dernley moved to strap Redel's feet. Unaware initially that the condemned man's feet were too far apart, he fumbled as he tried to secure the ankles and allowed the strap to fall. In a firm voice, Redel whispered to Dernley, 'Do your job properly!'

Dernley saw what the problem was, closed the man's feet together, and succeeded at his second attempt. Moments later the trap was sprung, and the two callous bank robbers, who had shot dead an innocent man in order to steal the paltry sum of just £28, paid with their lives.

For his heroic attempt to prevent the robbers escaping, Bob Taylor was later awarded the George Cross, the highest civilian award for bravery and heroism.

Records of an Execution carried out in		Prison on the 7 7 18 1950		
Particulars of the condemned Prisoner.	Particulars of the Execution.	Records respecting the Executioner and his Assistants (if any).		
		Name and Address, in full, of the Executioner.	Name and Address, in full, of the 1st Assistant to the Executioner (if any).	Name and Address, in full, of the 2nd Assistant to the Executioner (if any).
Zbigniew GOWER	The length of the drop, as determined before the execution. feet 6 inches 7	A. Pierrepoint 303 Manchester Rd Hollinwood Nr. Manchester Lancs.	Stephen Wade Eastdale Doncaster Rd Edenthorpe Nr Doncaster Yorks Sidney Dernley 10 Sherwood Rise Mansfield Woodhouse Mansfield, Notts.	Harry Kirk 4/0 Black Bones End Elton Peterborough Northants 3rd assistant Herbert Allen 352 Alwold Rd Selly Oak Birmingham
Prisoner Number 2006	The length of the drop, as measured after the execution, from the level of the floor of the scaffold to the heels of the suspended culprit. feet 6 inches 8¼			
Sex Male	Cause of death [(a) Dislocation of vertebræ, (b) Asphyxia.] Fracture dislocation between 3rd and 4th Cervical vertebrae with tearing of the cord.	Opinion of the Governor and Medical Officer as to the manner in which each of the above-named persons has performed his duty.		
Age 23		1. Has he performed his duty satisfactorily?	1.	1. 1. 1
Height 5'6"	Approximate statement of the character and amount of destruction to the soft and bony structures of the neck.	2. Was his general demeanour satisfactory during the period that he was in the prison, and does he appear to be a respectable person?	2.	2. 2. 2
Build Spare but muscular.	Fairly considerable bruising to soft tissues of neck but relatively little to skin, apart from bruise behind left ear. Bone damage entirely localised to site of fracture dislocation.	3. Has he shown capacity, both physical and mental, for the duty, and general suitability for the post?	3.	3. 3. 3
Weight in clothing (to be taken on the day preceding the execution) 150.		4. Is there any ground for supposing that he will bring discredit upon his office by lecturing, or by granting interviews to persons who may seek to elicit information from him in regard to the execution or by any other act?	4.	4. 4. 4
Character of the prisoner's neck Muscular, thick set.	If there were any peculiarities in the build or condition of the prisoner, or in the structure of his neck, which necessitated a departure from the scale of drops, particulars should be stated.	5. Are you aware of any circumstances occurring before, at, or after the execution which tend to show that he is not a suitable person to employ on future occasions either on account of incapacity for performing the duty, or the likelihood of his creating public scandal before or after an execution?	5.	5. 5. 5
		Marshall A.S. Fenton Gov		

LPC4 of bank robber Gower. (Author's Collection)

27

LOCKED IN THE MIND OF A MURDERER

William Edward Shaughnessy, 9 May 1951

Having already served several prison terms, including time in an approved school as a child, for a variety of petty crimes, mostly larceny, William Shaughnessy emigrated to Canada to try his luck overseas as the Depression and General Strike of the mid-1920s in his homeland made times hard. There he had married Marie Alexine, at Winnipeg in 1928, but he was deported back to England on 21 April 1933, following conviction and imprisonment for fraud and theft.

Arriving back in Portsmouth, he set up a shop buying and selling second-hand clothes at No. 319 Arundel Street, Landport, Portsmouth, while still dabbling in a life of crime, that was to land him with a number of further convictions before and after the Second World War, the last being in the summer of 1949. By this time his family had grown to six children, although the eldest daughters had married and moved away.

On Monday, 18 December 1950, Shaughnessy, now aged 48, spent the afternoon in several public houses around the town before returning home. Marie Shaughnessy was upstairs in the back bedroom with their 9-year-old daughter, Irene, and no sooner had Shaughnessy entered the house than he sent the young girl to the post office to buy him a 2½d stamp. Irene soon returned and found the back door of the shop on the latch and she was unable to gain entry without knocking. When her father came down he sent her back out saying he needed another stamp and he again locked the door. Irene was forced to go on two more errands, once to buy a postal order and finally to the baker's to buy some buns.

When Irene was finally let into the house she asked where her mother was and Shaughnessy told her she had gone to London with relatives who had come over from Canada on holiday. That night, Shaughnessy gave Irene and her brother Billy a few pennies so they could go to the pictures, while he took his 16-year-old son, Ronald, and 20-year-old daughter Joyce, out to several public houses, telling them he was celebrating a visit from his brother.

On the following day he told the youngest of the children that as they were off school for the Christmas holidays he was taking them to London, where they would meet up with their mother. There was no sign of their mother in London and on the

Left: *319 Arundel Street Portsmouth, where Shaughnessy kept a clothes shop. (Author's Collection)*

Below: *William Shaughnessy. (T.J. Leech Archive)*

Thursday, 16-year-old Ronnie returned to Portsmouth alone. Entering his sister Joyce's room he was horrified to find her lying in bed dead. He called the police who also discovered the body of Marie Shaughnessy concealed in a cupboard beneath the stairs. They in turn called in Scotland Yard, who hurried to Brighton with noted pathologist Dr Keith Simpson. Simpson told detectives that both women had been dead for several days, and in his opinion Mrs Shaughnessy had been dead longer than her daughter. In the case of the mother she had been battered about the head and strangled, while Joyce had been strangled with a stocking.

The hunt for Shaughnessy ended two days later and, taken into custody, he denied any involvement in the death of either his wife or daughter. As is the custom, when he stood trial before Mr Justice Byrne at Hampshire Assizes in March 1951, Shaughnessy faced only one charge of murder, in this case that of his 46-year-old wife.

Prosecution Counsel J. Scott Henderson KC claimed that although there was no clear motive for the crime other than a suggestion that they had quarrelled over unpaid rent money, it appeared that something had happened that caused Shaughnessy to kill his wife. He manufactured a situation where they were alone together by repeatedly sending his daughter on errands, and during that time he quarrelled with his wife causing him to attack her.

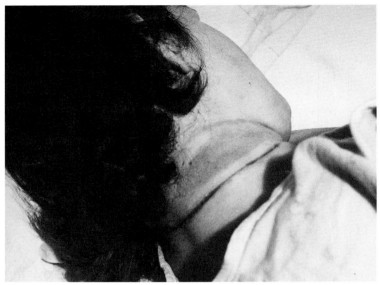

Above left: *Joyce Shaughnessy. (T.J. Leech Archive)*

Above right: *A close-up of the strangulation marks on Joyce Shaughnessy's neck. (TNA PRO)*

The prosecution claimed that he had attacked her with a weapon causing ten wounds to her face before strangling her with two stockings, using the time his daughter was out of the house to clear up the bloodstains and conceal her body in a cupboard beneath the stairs at their home.

Defence counsel E.E.S. Montagu told the court that Shaughnessy pleaded his innocence, and suggested that the real killer was probably the unidentified murderer that detectives in Portsmouth had been searching for in a case the press had dubbed 'The Red Sandals Murder' (in which a woman had been killed on the bombsite behind Shaughnessy's shop, and which was to remain unsolved). The prisoner claimed that he had returned home and found his wife dead and, in a panic, he had decided to hide the body and sent Irene out a number of times, so that 'the nipper would not be distressed at the sight'.

Scott Henderson again referred to the accused's lack of motive suggesting that it was possible for a motive to remain locked in the mind of a murderer and that a lack of a motive was no real defence in a charge of murder. The prisoner was unable to offer any reasonable explanation as to why he had not called the police instead of taking the children to London, where he promised them they would see their mother, when he knew she was already dead.

On 13 March, after a trial lasting four days, the jury took one hour and forty minutes, which included a break for lunch, to decide that Shaughnessy had been responsible for the death of his wife.

The murder of Joyce Shaughnessy remained on file.

28

THE LEFT-HANDED KILLER

Michael George Tatum, 14 May 1959

Capt. Charles Frederick Barrett had led a full and interesting life. Born in 1873, at the age of 17 he sailed to South Africa where he studied at a missionary college until the Zulu uprising and the outbreak of the Boer War caused him to abandon his studies and enlist into the British Army. Serving in the cavalry he rose through the ranks and when the Boer War ended in 1902 he returned to his homeland and settled in Maidstone where, besides breeding horses, he became an accomplished amateur steeplechaser.

When the First World War broke out in the summer of 1914 he rejoined the army. Amongst his military achievements he was the railhead commander in Salonika before joining the newly formed Royal Flying Corp. Following the armistice, his travels took him to Ireland where he ran a fishing hotel in Galway before he settled into retirement in Southampton.

His home at 11 Belmont Road, in the Portswood district of the city, was filled with numerous souvenirs of his travels with many items displayed on the walls in the lounge and hallway. Pride of place went to a Zulu knobkerrie, a hard wooden club, made of teak, given to Barrett by the novelist H. Rider Haggard whom he had met in his youth out in South Africa.

In December 1958, at the age of 85, he secured the services of a housekeeper to help with the running of the neat semi-detached house. The person appointed was 25-year-old Theresa Tatum, who moved into the house along with her husband Michael, a 24-year-old unemployed cinema projectionist.

Capt. Barrett occupied rooms on the ground and first floor; a tenant named Finn rented another room, with the Tatums sharing the other bedroom. Although Michael Tatum had been out of work when his wife took the role as a housekeeper, within a short time he found work with a local tyre manufacturer. However, on 9 January 1959 he lost this job and when he returned to Belmont Road he quarrelled with his wife to the extent that he packed his bags and moved out, taking lodgings a few streets away on Cambridge Road.

Capt. Barrett's home on Belmont Road, Southampton. (Author's Collection)

At 7 p.m. on Thursday night, 15 January 1959, lodger Finn left the house to go to work on the nightshift. Returning home at 7.30 a.m. the following morning, he found the front door open. This was unusual. When Finn walked down the passageway and up the stairs he found the door to Capt. Barrett's bedroom open and, looking inside, he discovered the battered and unconscious body of his landlord.

The emergency services were quickly summoned and while the old soldier was taken to hospital detectives examined the house for clues to his attacker. Found on the bedroom floor was the bloodstained Zulu knobkerrie which it seemed the attacker had lifted from the wall in the hallway. A dusty outline of where the club had been displayed was clear for the detectives to see. It seemed that Barrett had been struck repeatedly with the club, and when he died from his injuries later that day it became a murder hunt.

As there was no sign of a forced entry, detectives focused their enquiries on anyone holding a key to the house and this soon led them to Michael Tatum. Taken in for questioning, Tatum initially claimed that he had spent the night of the attack drinking in various pubs. He said a man he knew only as Derek, who had loaned him £7 that evening, could substantiate his alibi.

The dust outline shows where the murder weapon was removed from the wall. (TNA PRO)

Murder weapon was a gift from Rider Haggard

"Echo" Crime Reporter

THE weapon—a Zulu knobkerrie—with which Capt. Charles Barrett was murdered was a gift to him from H. Rider Haggard.

Capt. Barrett met the famous author of South African tales, writer of "She" and "King Solomon's Mines," when he was in South Africa, as a young man.

Was it the original club of the great Zulu Umslopogaas, Haggard's character of fiction, loyal friend of the Great White Hunter, Allan Quartermain? The Zulu was, some say, a real person whom Haggard himself had met.

The club was hanging on the wall in the hall of the Belmont-road house at Portswood, among a collection of South African trophies, when Capt. Barrett's murderer snatched it to creep upstairs—to steal a wallet with £ in it.

ZULU RISING

Capt. Barrett, born in 1873, went to South Africa to a missionary college to train as a missionary at the age of 17—in 1890.

A Zulu rising—and then the outbreak of the Boer War—led him to join the Army.

When he came home from South Africa he settled at Maidstone, became a breeder of horses, an amateur steeplechaser and a well known four-in-hand whip.

The First World War took him back to the Army—he was railhead commander in Salonika and later with the Royal Flying Corps

In other pages

TV and Radio 3
Topics of the Hour, Crossword 4
Racing selections 8

Capt. Barrett

A news cutting of the Knobkerrie murder. (Author's Collection)

Above left: *Michael George Tatum*. (*Author's Collection*)

Above right: *Hangman Robert Leslie 'Jock' Stewart carried out the last two executions at Winchester.* (*Author's Collection*)

When officers failed to trace this man Tatum changed his story and admitted that he had gone to the house to speak to his wife. He claimed a friend, Terence Richard 'Terry' Thatcher, had accompanied him, and that once inside the house the two men decided to commit robbery. Tatum admitted he had entered the bedroom and stolen a wallet, but said it had been Thatcher who had removed the knobkerrie from the wall and used it to batter the old man.

Asked to describe his accomplice, Tatum was able to give few scant details, but although detectives were able to trace a Terence Thatcher he quickly established that he had no connection with Tatum and was able to prove that he had been nowhere near Southampton on the night of the attack. When confronted with this Tatum simply claimed it was a different Terry Thatcher.

On 18 January, Londoner Tatum was formally charged with capital murder in the furtherance of theft and stood trial on 19 March at the Hampshire Assizes, in Winchester.

Following a number of high-profile murder cases in the early 1950s in which the press and general public felt the death penalty was proving to be inconsistent and in need of a review, the government decided to hold an enquiry – and as a result, in 1957 they passed the Homicide Act, which categorised murder into capital and non-capital. Only the former carried the death penalty. Capital murder was limited to just a handful of offences and included the murder of a policeman, murder using a firearm and murder during the furtherance of theft.

Prosecution Counsel Norman Skelhorn KC outlined the case, stating that Capt. Barrett had been struck three times with the wooden Zulu club and had died of a fractured skull. The accused had admitted the theft of Barrett's wallet and as a result he had committed capital murder. The evidence also suggested that the murder weapon had been wielded by a left-handed killer; the accused was left handed.

Defence Counsel, E.S. Fay KC told the court that the defence was two-fold. The accused was not denying his involvement in the murder but denied he played any part in the violence inflicted on the old man, which had been carried out, he contested, by an accomplice. Therefore the first plea was a defence of manslaughter, on the grounds of diminished responsibility.

A doctor called by the defence claimed that Tatum was an 'incipient schizophrenic', but doctors called by the prosecution refuted this by stating that while Tatum was certainly abnormal, it did not impair his mental responsibility. They also claimed that Tatum was a compulsive liar, lived in a fantasy world and boasted and made claims which he believed would enhance other people's opinion of him. At various times he claimed to have been an officer in the Australian navy, a police officer and invented stories of sporting achievements and the trophies he'd won for various events. On one occasion he had even told bosses at his place of work that his wife had died; colleagues had even organised a collection for a wreath. However, she later turned up at the workplace, very much alive!

On Monday 23 March the jury of nine men and three women needed just forty minutes to return a verdict of guilty of capital murder and Mr Justice Cassels, who celebrated his 82nd birthday during the trial, passed sentence of death. Tatum's appeal was dismissed on Monday 27 April, and on Thursday 14 May he became the eleventh man to be hanged following the passing of the Homicide Act.

Unlike the previous execution, that of police-killer Ronald Marwood at Pentonville eight days before, which had attracted massive public interest with police on horseback breaking up rioting demonstrators outside the north London gaol, Tatum's execution was very low key. Newspapers recorded that a solitary man approached the large green prison gates as the fateful moment approached and, as a clock chimed the hour, he removed his cap and stood in silence.

29

FOR FOUR POUNDS

'Nanjarrow' a rural farmhouse close to the village of Constantine, seven miles from Falmouth, Devon, had kept a secret for over forty years. By the summer of 1963, its sole occupant, William Garfield Rowe, had been on the run – a deserter – from his unit since the latter days of the First World War. Rowe had been conscripted in 1916, at the age of 18, but had fled from his unit one week later, and although he was soon captured, he once again managed to escape and, fearful of the repercussions if taken back into custody, for the next thirty-five years he was shielded by his family hiding on his parent's farm in the Cornish fishing village of Porthleven, then latterly at Nanjarrow. Neighbours were told he had been killed in action fighting in France.

Following her coronation in 1953, Queen Elizabeth II granted a pardon to all deserters and although 'Willy' Rowe was now technically a free man, so set in his routine was he now that he rarely left the farm unless it was dark, having become a hermit and recluse whose only pleasure was studying the language of Esperanto.

To say his reappearance into the village was a shock would be an understatement. When his mother passed away family friends and neighbours were stunned to find Rowe dressed in his mourning clothes at her graveside and from then on he gradually began to have contact with outsiders and do business from the farm.

Nanjarrow was a very basic farmhouse – there was no running water, plumbing or sanitation – but he managed to run the farm well enough to make a living, so much so that it was rumoured locally that he was a wealthy man and there had even been a robbery at Nanjarrow in 1961.

On Thursday morning, 15 August 1963, agricultural salesman Henry Pascoe called at Nanjarrow where he had an appointment with Willy Rowe. As he made his way up the path he could tell from the sound of the cows that they were late being milked. Finding no reply to his knocking at the front door he walked around to the back of farmhouse – where he discovered the old man's body lying close to a wall. He had died from severe head injuries, and his throat had been cut.

Opposite: *Willy Rowe's body outside the farmhouse at Nanjarrow. (TNA PRO)*

Detectives were soon at the farm and a doctor confirmed that Rowe had been stabbed several times: there were five stab wounds in the chest, two in the neck, and one in the side of the head. A check of his movements found he had last been seen alive at 9.15 p.m. on the previous evening and they believed he had been killed during the course of a robbery. It was thought that over £3,000 had been stolen, and the inside of the farmhouse had been ransacked, seemingly as the killer had searched for the money.

The Chief Constable of Cornwall, R.B. Matthews immediately called in Scotland Yard and Detective Superintendent Maurice Osborn, with his sergeant, Andrew McPhee, arrived to take over the investigation. One of the first things local officers put into place was a roadblock around Constantine questioning car owners and passengers. On the following day they stopped a motorcyclist. He gave his name as 23-year-old John Pascoe and said that, having separated from his young wife and their child, he shared a caravan with another young man, 22-year-old Dennis Whitty, and three teenage girls, fourteen miles away on the outskirts of Truro.

When questioned by officers, Pascoe – whose real name was actually Russell, although he was known to family and friends as John – admitted he knew Willy Rowe and, that after leaving school, he had once spent the summer working on the farm. When the officers had a briefing later that day and discussed information that had so far come to

hand, Scotland Yard detectives learned from local police that Pascoe's parents lived in Constantine and that two years earlier Willy Rowe had told officers investigating the robbery at Nanjarrow that he suspected John Pascoe, who had just finished working on the farm, of being involved. Local officers had followed this up but no charges were ever pressed.

Armed with this information, detectives travelled to the caravan near Truro and invited the two men and three girls, Esha Sweeney, Brigit Hamilton and Norma Booker, all nineteen, to Falmouth police station to help with their inquiries. Once the girls were questioned police soon learned that on the Wednesday night the two men had left Truro on Pascoe's motorcycle claiming they had a job to do, and that when they returned in the early hours both had been in a highly excited and agitated state.

Norma Booker said the men had gone armed with an iron bar, knife, and starting pistol and following their return Pascoe seemed distraught, while Whitty seemed exuberant and boastful. Whitty had then told her that he would kill any of them if they talked.

Following the girls' statements, which each corroborated the other, the men were questioned and soon broke down. Whitty confessed that they had called at the farmhouse at 11 p.m., pretending to be helicopter pilots who had crashed nearby and asking to use a telephone. A similar incident had happened a few months before and had been reported

Inside the ransacked living room. (TNA PRO)

Right: *Det. Supt. Maurice Osborn who led the enquiry into the Nanjarrow murder. (Crime Picture Archive)*

Below: *The police sketch of Nanjarrow. (TNA PRO)*

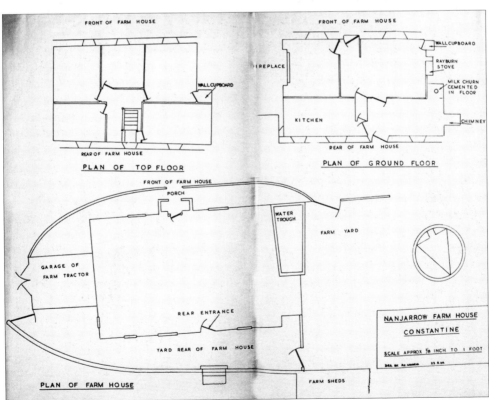

in the local press. He said that Pascoe had then hit Rowe with an iron bar.

Questioning soon suggested to the experienced detectives that Whitty, although the younger of the two, was the leader and that Pascoe was merely the accomplice. Pascoe admitted that he had hit the old man over the head once, with the iron bar, but he had merely watched as Whitty 'went berserk with the knife ...'

He then made a statement in which he admitted:

We went on my motorbike, and knocked on the farmhouse door at about 11 o'clock. Old man Rowe answered the door. Dennis was standing in front of the door and said he was a helicopter pilot, and had crashed, and wanted to use the 'phone. I then hit Rowe on the back of the head, with a small iron-bar. I meant only to knock him out, that's all. Whitty took the iron-bar and went for him. I had to walk away honest, I did. I went inside and found £4 under a piano. Dennis took a watch and two big boxes of matches, and some keys from the old man's pockets. We shared the £4, and I've spent mine... I didn't kill him! That was my mate. He went mad, he did. I didn't stop him, in fear he would stick me. I had to walk away. I couldn't stop him. He said he finished him when he stuck him with the knife in his throat. I only knocked him on the head with a bar. I just knocked him out.

Confronted with this Whitty countered by claiming Pascoe had made him stab Rowe. 'I stabbed him in the chest. Pascoe was going to hit me, so I stuck him (Rowe) in the neck.'

At Cornwall Assizes, Bodmin, before Mr Justice Thesinger, on Monday 3 November 1963, both Pascoe and Whitty were charged with capital murder, in the furtherance of theft. The prosecution's case was built firmly on the confessions both had made to Scotland Yard detectives and in the courtroom both counsels tried to put the onus on the other accused. Both had pleaded not guilty to murder, by virtue of admitting manslaughter, on the grounds of diminished responsibility.

Outlining the case for the prosecution, John Wood QC, described the murder as '...one of the most horrible and gruesome known in this county or country.' He said it was clear that Whitty was the leader who had planned the attack, caused the fatal wounds and threatened the others if they 'grassed'. Whitty's counsel, Norman Brodick QC, countered this by telling the court that three years earlier Pascoe had burgled Rowe, stealing £200, together with some of his deceased mother's jewellery, and had suggested they target the farm again. With the evidence and witnesses suggesting that Whitty had intended to kill Rowe, in Pascoe's case all the Crown had to do was show he intended to cause Rowe grievous bodily harm; even if he did not intend this, his mere presence at the scene while Whitty killed the old man was enough to convict him of the capital charge. The jury clearly agreed and on 3 November, after a five-day trial, they were deemed equally guilty and, convicted of capital murder in the furtherance of theft, both were sentenced to death.

Removed from the dock, the men were only to see each other once more, at their failed appeal at the Court of Criminal Appeal in London on Tuesday 25 November. When Home Secretary Henry Brooke announced he could not order a reprieve,

3 CARAVAN GIRLS TELL OF MURDER NIGHT

By REG SCOTT

THREE 19-year-old girls living in a caravan with two men told a court of murder confessions yesterday.

Norma Booker, of Lewham - road, Truro, Cornwall, said one of the men, Russell Pascoe, 23, told her that "If we opened our mouths we would end up the same way."

'Men who lived with us confessed'

near Falmouth, on August 14.

The killers had ransacked the house. They got away with £4, but missed £3,000 hidden there.

Pascoe, of Constantine, and Whitty, of St. Keverne, are accused of murdering

meant to just knock him out, that's all. I said to Dennis: 'Let it go at that,' but he went mad with the knife and took the bar from me and kept thumping him on the head."

Mr. Wood told the court that in a statement Whitty

said: "Pascoe hit him with the bar, and he said to me: 'Go on, stick him.'

"I didn't want to. He said he would use the bar on me if I didn't do it. So I stuck the knife into the old man's chest, three or four times, and in the

throat, I was crying all the time."

Esha Sweeney, of Devoran, told the court that Pascoe said: "We had to do it because the farmer recognised me."

Bridget Hamilton, of Penance-lane, Lanner, said Whitty had confessed to her.

The case goes on today.

Russell Pascoe   *Dennis Whitty*

Above: *A newspaper report of the trial of Whitty and Pascoe. (Crime Picture Archive)*

Below: *Dennis Whitty, the last man hanged at Winchester. (Author's Collection)*

there was uproar in the Commons. Government ministers refused to discuss the case and members of the opposition, both Labour and Liberal MPs, hurled handbills towards the Conservative side of the house and jeered. Whitty's fiancée was the subject of media interest as she visited him on the eve of his execution, being photographed in tears as she was driven away from Winchester in a taxi. At 9 a.m., on Tuesday 17 December, Whitty walked to the gallows at Winchester while at Bristol Prison John Pascoe faced the same fate.

The futility of Pascoe and Whitty's crime is perhaps best summed up by the haul the brutal crime yielded. Although it was originally believed that over £3,000 had been stolen, officers discovered a map with instructions written in Esperanto amongst papers found in the house. When this was translated it lead detectives to a spot in the cowshed where a safe was hidden containing several thousand pounds; another map contained directions to a hiding place in the farmyard where, buried in a shallow grave, they found a glass jar packed with bank notes.

Dennis Whitty and John Pascoe were hanged for the meagre sum of just £4.

APPENDIX I

PUBLIC EXECUTIONS OUTSIDE WINCHESTER GAOL

1800 – 1867

Date	Convict	Crime	Executioner
17 March 1800	Juan Barugo	Murdered a shipmate at sea	
17 March 1800	John Diggins	Highway Robbery	
12 March 1804	Elizabeth Cazsar	Murder of her bastard son	
12 March 1804	John Gubby (20)	Murder of William Harben	
12 March 1804	John Harben (21)	Murder of his father William Harben	
26 March 1808	Louis Herquidda	Murdered a fellow prisoner of war	
24 March 1810	Rebecca Blundell	Murdered for gain	
13 July 1812	John William James	Murdered his girlfriend on the Isle of Wight	
14 March 1814	Jean Louis Sere	Stabbed a man at Gosport	
14 March 1814	Jean Marie Danre	Stabbed a man at Gosport	
14 March 1814	Francois Recit	Stabbed a man at Gosport	
11 March 1816	James McKean	Murdered a man on the Isle of Wight	
11 March 1816	Antonio Picque	Murdered Dilly Jerome at Portsea	
11 March 1816	Joseph Picque		
9 March 1818	Hugh Flynn	Stabbed fellow Irish workmate at Titchfield	
8 March 1819	Sarah Huntingford (69)	Murdered her husband at Portsea	
10 March 1828	Moses Shepherd (18)	Murdered a man at Fareham	
3 August 1829	John Stacey	House breaking at Portsmouth	

July 1830	William Brown	Beat a fellow prisoner to death with a hammer at Wisney	
July 1830	Smith Williams	Beat a fellow prisoner to death with a hammer at Wisney	
March 1834	William Rose (74)	Murdered his wife	
July 1836	John Deadman (60)	Robbed a postman at Bishop's Sutton	
August 1848	William Atter	Murdered a prison officer at Portsmouth Dockyard	
January 1856	Abraham Baker (26)	Shot dead his girlfriend at Southampton	
March 1856	Thomas Charles Jones (46)	Murdered prison doctor onboard ship in Portsmouth Harbour	
December 1856	Guiseppe Lagava (20)	Murdered a naval officer at sea	
December 1856	Giovanni Bartelano (18)	Murdered a naval officer at sea	
December 1856	Matteo Pettrick (21)	Murdered a naval officer at sea	
January 1861	James Jackson (25)	Shot dead his sergeant at Aldershot	
December 1861	Thomas Jackson (19)	Shot dead his sergeant at Aldershot	
August 1862	George Jacob Gilbert (30)	Rape and murder at Fordingbridge	
December 1862	Fernando Petrina (26)	Murdered ship's captain at sea	William Calcraft
August 1865	John Hughes (21)	Murdered a prostitute at Portsmouth	William Calcraft
December 1867	Frederick Baker (29)	Murdered 'Sweet' Fanny Adams at Alton	William Calcraft

APPENDIX II

PRIVATE EXECUTIONS AT WINCHESTER GAOL

1869 - 1963

Date	Convict	Executioner	Assistant (s)
6 September 1869	William Dixon	William Marwood	None Engaged
16 November 1874	Thomas Smith	William Marwood	None Engaged
11 February 1878	James Caffyn	William Marwood	None Engaged
31 May 1886+	Albert Edward Brown	James Berry	None Engaged
31 May 1886	James Whelan		
27 March 1888	George Clarke	James Berry	None Engaged
26 August 1891	Edward Henry F. Watts	James Billington	None Engaged
6 December 1893	George Mason	James Billington	None Engaged
18 July 1894	Samuel Elkins	James Billington	None Engaged
12 December 1894+	Cyrus Knight	James Billington	William Wilkinson
12 December 1894	William Rogers		
21 July 1896	Phillip Mathews	James Billington	William Wilkinson
21 July 1896	Frederick Burden		
21 July 1896	Samuel Edward Smith		
18 July 1899	Charles Maidment	James Billington	None Engaged
22 July 1902	William Churcher	William Billington	None Engaged
16 December 1903	William Brown	William Billington	John Billington
16 December 1903	Thomas Cowdrey		
26 November 1913	Augustus John Penny	John Ellis	Albert Lumb^
16 June 1914	Walter James White	John Ellis	Thomas Pierrepoint
29 March 1917	Leo George O'Donnell	John Ellis	Robert Baxter

19 August 1922	Thomas Henry Allaway	John Ellis	Edward Taylor
30 July 1924	Abraham Goldenberg	Thomas Pierrepoint	William Willis
12 August 1926	Charles Edward Finden	Thomas Pierrepoint	Robert Baxter
22 April 1930	William Henry Podmore	Thomas Pierrepoint	Alfred Allen
28 July 1949	Sydney A. F. Chamberlain	Albert Pierrepoint	Harry B. Allen
7 July 1950	Zbigniew Gower	Albert Pierrepoint	Harry Kirk
7 July 1950	Roman Redel	Sydney Dernley	Herbert Allen
9 May 1951	William E. Shaughnessy	Albert Pierrepoint	Harry B. Allen
14 May 1959	Michael George Tatum	Robert L. Stewart	Thomas Cunliffe
17 December 1963	Dennis John Whitty	Robert L. Stewart	Harry F. Robinson

+ signifies a double execution of prisoners not connected and hanged for separate crimes

signifies a triple execution of prisoners not connected and hanged for separate crimes

^ Lumb's names is noted in LPC4 book but is crossed out and no record of his conduct noted. This suggests he was engaged but not present at the actual execution.

INDEX